Jwalking

A Guide to Following Jesus
for New and Growing Christians

DR. ARNOLD R. FLEAGLE

SONFIRE MEDIA
A PUBLISHING COMPANY
GALAX, VIRGINIA

J-Walking: A Guide to Following Jesus for New and
Growing Christians

Published by Sonfire Media, LLC
PO Box 6
Galax, VA 24333 USA

Publisher's Note: The author wishes to capitalize deity pronouns and has made this change in Scripture quotations within this book.

Cover and interior book design by Larry W. VanHoose

ISBN No. 978-0-9891064-7-4

Dedication

I dedicate this book to Rev. Kenschaft, Rev. North, and three laymen, David Hippensteel, Harry Sollensberger, and Alfred Woltz who taught me the Bible at a young age and demonstrated how to convert theology into biology. I seek now to make the invisible Christ visible before my family, my flock, and the world.

Table of Contents

Acknowledgments

My special gratitude is extended to my wife, Faye, for her support of my writing endeavors; to my son, Matthew, for his valuable insights; to David Fessenden and Vie Herlocker for their investment in editing this work; and to Beth Brister, Tami Fly, and Tammy Neighbour, for their secretarial skills, which greatly enhanced the project.

FOREWORD

I have had the privilege of knowing Dr. Arnold Fleagle for a number of years and of serving alongside him as his associate pastor for three. Before joining his pastoral staff, I used his book *Broken Windows of the Soul* with my accountability partner, and found it insightful and helpful.

I learned firsthand that "Pastor Arnie" has a desire to see spiritually lost people become not only believers in Jesus, but followers of Jesus too. He does not want any believer to live as a casual Christian, but as a committed Christian, who lives, loves, and leads like Jesus. He has tried to personally live like Jesus and disciple others to do the same.

This book is part of Dr. Fleagle's desire, and is an overflow of his life. Everything he wrote about in *J-Walking*, he has and is living out personally. It is a life of joy, purpose, service, discipline, and discovery of the deep well that is Jesus.

My calling is to work with Christian ministry leaders across the country with Sonlife Ministries, equipping them to walk like Jesus and make disciples as Jesus did. *J-Walking* is a valuable tool I will pass on to these leaders. As they build ministries by helping spiritually lost people become believers, *J-Walking* will serve as a great resource to help these new believers grow in their walk with Jesus to become mature workers in His harvest field.

So if you are a new believer, pick up this book and begin growing in your new relationship with Jesus. If you have been a follower of Jesus for a while, this is a great book for you to go through personally to take you deeper, and then take someone else through it, helping to disciple them as you become a disciple-maker. Don't settle for just believing in Jesus or knowing about Jesus. Dig into this book to truly understand Him and live like Him. Leave a legacy for Him as you walk like Jesus!

Rev. Joel Zaborowski
Associate Director of Leadership Development
Sonlife Ministries
www.sonlife.com

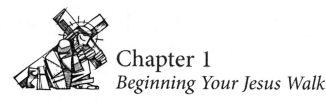

Chapter 1
Beginning Your Jesus Walk

A Note from the Author to Help You Get Started

Before Jesus ascended into heaven He left this Great Command or Commission: "Therefore go and make disciples of all nations, baptizing them in the name of the Father and of the Son and of the Holy Spirit, and teaching them to obey everything I have commanded you. And surely I am with you always, to the very end of the age" (Matthew 28:19-20).

Two particular details stand out to me, first, we are to make disciples and, second, we are to teach them.

J-Walking, or *Jesus Walking*, is a manual for brand new Christians or those growing in faith. Its purpose is to help you become a devoted and fruitful disciple of Jesus Christ, a disciple who understands His teaching, and who patterns your life after the template that Jesus left us.

When Jesus issued the invitation in Matthew 4:19 to "Follow Me," He proceeded to impact His followers' lives through His lips and His lifestyle. The ground He covered with His followers embraced not only the content of His teaching but also the expectation that they would be imitators of Him.

J-Walking presents themed chapters to help you better understand and follow Jesus. These themes range from foundational topics such as prayer, studying the Bible, and worship, to nontraditional topics such as anger, social media, and how to select a translation of the Bible. Each chapter begins with a question and a short Bible passage related to the theme. Within each chapter, you'll find additional Scripture and commentary to help you engage with and apply the information in your own life. While many themes are related, the chapters stand alone, allowing you to peruse topically or read chronologically.

Simply put, If Jesus is the master copy, then all other copies (His disciples) should look a lot like the Master. In *J-Walking*, my desire is to cultivate both right belief with right living. If this is achieved in some, most, or all of the areas considered, then this book has been worth the effort, and more importantly, it has accomplished the directive of Jesus to *follow Him* and *make disciples that make disciples.*

Soli Deo Gloria
(To God Alone Be the Glory)

Arnold R. Fleagle

Chapter 2
New Life as a Christian

What happens to me when I accept Jesus as my Lord and Savior?

What the Bible Has to Say

Yet to all who received Him [Jesus], to those who believed in His name, He gave the right to become children of God. (John 1:12)

Life is a series of moments. Some moments hold more significance than others, such as the day we are born, the first day of school, the day we are married, the day our first child is born, and the day of our death. These moments are landmarks in our life and legacy. However, the day we receive Jesus Christ as our Lord and Savior is the most strategic moment of our earthly journey. On that day we exchange our sins for His salvation, trade our old life for a new life, and give up our independence from Him for a lifestyle of dependence on Him.

One college girl remarked that when she became a Christian she felt like she had swallowed sunshine. C.S. Lewis, an atheist who became one of the most influential Christians of the twentieth century, entitled his autobiography, *Surprised by Joy*. He described his conversion to Jesus Christ as: "I felt as if I were a man of snow at long last starting to melt." That night Lewis wrote, "I gave in, and admitted that God was God, and knelt and prayed: perhaps that night, the most dejected and reluctant convert in all England."

Now that you are a follower of Jesus Christ and have received new life, you have been provided with a whole list of benefits. The moment you accepted God's offer of salvation, many events took place:

- God adopted you as His child (Ephesians 1:5)

- He forgave your sins and does not hold them against you (Hebrews 8:12)

- He washed your heart whiter than snow (Isaiah 1:18)

- He wrote your name in the Lamb's Book of Life (Revelation 21:27)

- He entered your heart and took up residence through His Holy Spirit (Acts 2:37–38)

- He gives you an inheritance in heaven (Ephesians 1:13–14)

- He considers you a new creature (2 Corinthians 5:17)

I want to encourage you with these truths: God loves you with an everlasting love, and He will provide for, protect, and purify His children.

As you grow in the Lord, feed on His Word daily, get involved in a small group of Christians who meet to learn more about Christ, and be faithful to morning worship. If the church you are attending has a new believers' class or foundations class, sign up. These things will provide you with a basic introduction to the Christian faith.

Think About It

When Nicodemus, a Jewish ruler, visited Jesus, our Lord said to him, "No one can see the kingdom of God unless he is born again" (John 3:3). When Paul spoke of the person who came to Jesus and became His follower he described it like this: "Therefore, if anyone is in Christ, he is a new creation; the old has gone, the new has come!" (2 Corinthians 5:17). When you initially become a Christian you are like a newborn child. Remember this: a baby has no prior history. Everything is new.

What This Means to You

Many aspects of your life changed the moment you accepted Jesus. Go forward in your new faith. As my eye doctor once told me, "Don't keep looking through the rearview mirror at the past; look through the front windshield and move ahead into a new future."

Chapter 3
Assurance of Salvation

*How can I know I am truly forgiven, saved from my sins,
and a part of God's family?*

What the Bible Has to Say

*Because I know whom I have believed, and am convinced that
He is able to guard what I have entrusted to Him for that day.*
(2 Timothy 1:12)

The assurance of your salvation is grounded in the person of Jesus Christ and the promises of God's Word. Robert Cook wrote, "Salvation is not something you do, but something Christ does when you receive Him" (*Now That I Believe*, p. 13). The theme verse, 2 Timothy 1:12, displays Paul's absolute confidence in the reality of his salvation. His belief is grounded in Jesus Christ and in our Lord's ability to guard and protect what Paul had given Him. Can we expect to have such a high level of trust as Paul apparently possessed? I believe the answer is yes.

The New Testament provides many Scriptures which create such a rock-solid confidence. John 1:12 conveys how a person receives Jesus Christ: "Yet to all who received Him, to those who believed in His name, He gave the right to become children of God." The emphasis of the verses is Jesus. His name means "the Lord saves." When we receive or accept Him, we have a change of status: we become children of God. We enter God's family. This is not based on our authority or wishes; it is based upon the authority of Jesus Christ Himself.

How have you been saved—that is, rescued from your position as a sinner, which has a penalty—and given a new status in Jesus Christ? Ephesians 2:8–9 takes this salvation reality out of your hands and out of your performance. "For it is by grace you have been saved, through faith—and this not from yourselves, it is the gift of God—not by works, so that no one can boast." These two verses form a basic tenant of our faith: our salvation is achieved apart from our actions and deeds. God gives us a gift—and a gift is not earned, it is received. This gift is given because of God's grace. And grace is defined as "the unmerited favor of God." Grace is not earned or deserved, but is given despite who we are or what we have done. We can take assurance in a work done by the Creator and Sustainer of our universe.

Another significant Scripture that points to our concrete and certain salvation is found in 1 John 5:11–12: "And this is the testimony: God has given us eternal life, and this life is in His Son. He who has the Son has life; he who does not have the Son does not have life." These verses are God's testimony; He always tells the truth, and He is the truth. What kind of life does He give? Life eternal, everlasting, without end. Who has this type of never-ending life? The person who accepts this gift of Jesus Christ, the Son, is the recipient of a gift beyond our ability to comprehend. However, if a person declines this gift and does not accept and receive Jesus Christ as Lord and Savior, then that person does not have eternal life.

Romans 6:23 adds to our understanding of the "haves" and "have nots" regarding the assurance of being saved. This verse tells us that sin pays: "For the wages of sin is death [in other words, our actions and deeds have earned us a negative dividend, that is, death], but the gift of God is eternal life in Christ Jesus our Lord." Again, our assurance is based on what God has given us, not what we have earned. The "miniature gospel," as it is called, John 3:16, gives further proof of this concept of a gift: "For God so loved the world that He *gave* His one and only Son, that whoever believes in Him shall not perish but have eternal life."

The theme is recurrent, *God loves us enough to give us a gift based on the work of His Son, not on our own personal résumé and achievements.* Your salvation, my salvation—everyone's salvation—is based upon the gift God gives to those who believe Jesus Christ dealt with our sins by dying on the cross, thereby canceling our debt and the penalties that are accumulated by our sins, including the final penalty, eternal death.

Think About It

You are standing at one end of a high bridge which crosses a raging river. Your friends are waving and shouting at you to cross the bridge and join them. As you attempt the crossing, which situation would you rather face—strong faith in a weak bridge, or weak faith in a strong bridge? Strong faith in a weak bridge will land you in the river, but weak faith in a strong bridge will land you on the other side. Jesus Christ is the bridge over troubled water—He will not fail you if you are willing to trust Him.

What This Means to You

The assurance of salvation solely rests on the gift of God and His Son, Jesus Christ. Your "blessed assurance" rests in the promises of God, which were purchased through the life, death, and resurrection of Jesus Christ. Be confident.

Chapter 4
Worship

How essential is it that I worship with other believers?

What the Bible Has to Say

Let us not give up meeting together, as some are in the habit of doing, but let us encourage one another—and all the more as we see the Day approaching. (Hebrews 10:25)

The writer to the Hebrews clearly puts worship in the plus column; perhaps we should say the *must* column. Christianity certainly has its individual aspects such as private prayer, fasting from food, and one-on-one witnessing. But the Bible also uses compelling word pictures to emphasize the corporate life of believers, such as the body of Christ (one body with many members) and the household of faith (many members make up one family). The Greek word for church, *ekklesia*, means "the called-out ones"—and it is plural, not singular.

The Jewish people moved forward in community throughout the Old Testament. They worshiped the God of Abraham, Isaac, and Jacob with great festivals such as Passover and Pentecost. When the journeys through the wilderness were taking place, they worshiped the Lord with a movable church called the tabernacle. Later they moved to stationary places of worship called temples, the most prestigious being Solomon's temple. The psalmist invited people to worship: "Come, let us bow down in worship, let us kneel before the LORD our maker" (Psalm 95:6). David's passionate heart for worshiping with other believers is displayed when he exclaimed, "I rejoiced with those who said to me, 'Let us go to the house of the Lord'" (Psalm 122:1).

A disciple of Jesus is one who follows in His footsteps. In fact, Jesus's call to the first group of disciples was, "Follow me" (Matthew 4:19). If we want to be like Him, we should notice He regularly went to the temple and to the local synagogue (a gathering place for worship). Luke 4:16 reports it as one of His habits: "And He came to Nazareth, where He had been brought up: and, as His custom was, He went into the synagogue on the Sabbath day, and stood up for to read" (KJV). His pattern should be our pattern. He was a frequent participant in worship and study opportunities.

Think About It

A.W. Tozer labeled worship, "The missing jewel of the evangelical church." He wrote in his book *The Knowledge of the Holy* that, "The concept of the majesty of God has all but disappeared from the human race" (p. 123). Worship is the first and foremost duty of a believer's life. We must pursue the personal and corporate worship of the Lord God Almighty. To neglect worship is to lose spiritual health and holiness.

What This Means to You

Make worship a consistent practice of your Christian walk.

Chapter 5
Baptism

What is the meaning of baptism?
Do I have to be baptized, or is it optional?

What the Bible Has to Say

When the people heard this, they were cut to the heart and said to Peter and the other apostles, "Brothers, what shall we do?" Peter replied, "Repent and be baptized, every one of you, in the name of Jesus Christ for the forgiveness of your sins. And you will receive the gift of the Holy Spirit. The promise is for you and your children and for all who are far off—for all whom the Lord our God will call." (Acts 2:37–39)

Water baptism is an act of commitment or dedication to God—a demonstration of faith which we call an *ordinance* or *sacrament*. By being baptized, a person is publicly declaring, "I have been cleansed by God and changed. I am now a follower of the Christian faith." Baptism is often described as an "outward sign of an inward work of grace." In other words, it is a way of outwardly declaring to the world what has happened in your heart.

Water symbolizes cleansing from sin. Believer's baptism takes place after a person repents of sin and trusts in Jesus. This is in contrast to infant baptism, which takes place shortly after birth, long before one can understand the need for a Savior and a personal commitment of faith in Jesus Christ.

There are three modes of baptism: *sprinkling,* or releasing drops of water over one's head; *pouring,* or running a stream of water over one's head, often with a pitcher; and *immersion,* or lowering one under water, then raising the person up out of the water.

Immersion is the mode which most clearly symbolizes the significance of baptism as recorded in Romans 6:3–4: "Or don't you know that all of us who were baptized into Christ Jesus were baptized into his death? We were therefore buried with him through baptism into death in order that, just as Christ was raised from the dead through the glory of the Father, we too may live a new life."

Immersion also fits with the root meaning of baptism, found in Greek words such as *bapto,* "to dip, dip into a dye, or draw water," and *baptizo,* "to dip, to cause to perish as by drowning a man or sinking a ship."

Several passages in the New Testament encourage baptism for believers; for example, there is Christ's command in Matthew 28:19: "Therefore go and make disciples of all nations, baptizing them in the name of the Father and of the Son and of the Holy Spirit." Christ's example is in Mark 1:9: "At that time Jesus came from Nazareth in Galilee and was baptized by John in the Jordan." After his dramatic Pentecostal message, Peter replied, "Repent and be baptized, every one of you, in the name of Jesus Christ for the forgiveness of your sins. And you will receive the gift of the Holy Spirit" (Acts 2:38). Even the apostle Paul was instructed to be baptized: "And now what are you waiting for? Get up, be baptized and wash your sins away, calling on his name" (Acts 22:16).

Finally, baptism is identification with Jesus Christ. Paul explains, "For all of you who were baptized into Christ have clothed yourselves with Christ" (Galatians 3:27).

Think About It

This final verse, Galatians 3:27, uses the phrase "baptism into Christ," which encompasses both your initial act of receiving Christ in faith, and your public baptism which testifies to others of your personal commitment to Him. The apostle Paul describes this as being clothed with Christ. Isn't that a striking metaphor?

You have probably heard the expression, "Dress for success." Many people depend on expensive clothing labels to upgrade their reputation and status before others. I looked up the ten most expensive clothing brands, and found that *Gucci* was number one. Some people will max out their credit cards to get a wardrobe from this designer.

The cost of Gucci, however, doesn't even come close to the price paid for you to be clothed with Christ. He offered His body to be broken and His blood to be shed so that when God the Father looked at you, He would not see your sinfulness, but His Son.

What This Means to You

Jesus, Peter, and Paul—all three—endorsed baptism as an integral part of the Christian faith. You should follow their example and exhortation and be baptized. Remember Peter's words: "Be baptized, every one of you."

Chapter 6
The Lord's Supper

What is the origin and meaning of the Lord's Supper, or Holy Communion? How is it relevant to my Christian faith and walk?

What the Bible Has to Say

For whenever you eat this bread and drink this cup, you proclaim the Lord's death until He comes. (1 Corinthians 11:26)

The Lord's Supper can be traced back to the Jewish Passover: "And when your children ask you, 'What does this ceremony mean to you?' then tell them, 'It is the Passover sacrifice to the Lord, who passed over the houses of the Israelites in Egypt and spared our homes when He struck down the Egyptians'" (Exodus 12:26, 27). Jesus was celebrating the Feast of Passover, also known as the Feast of Unleavened Bread, when He began the Lord's Supper.

There are two key symbols. The first is unleavened bread (flatbread, bread without yeast), eaten at the Lord's Supper. Exodus 12:8 reports, "That same night they are to eat the meat roasted over the fire, along with bitter herbs, and bread made without yeast." Exodus 12:39 explains further: "With the dough they had brought from Egypt, they baked cakes of unleavened bread. The dough was without yeast because they had been driven out of Egypt and *did not have time* to prepare food for themselves." The bread symbolized the *quickness* of their escape from the bondage of Egypt. Jesus, as He held up the unleavened bread of His Last Supper, told His disciples, "This is my body, which is for you; do this in remembrance of me" (1 Corinthians 11:24).

A second symbol was a year-old lamb, without defect, that was sacrificed. The command is found in Exodus 12:7: "Then they are to take some of the blood and put it on the sides and tops of the doorframes of the houses where they eat the lambs." The next verse states, "That same night they are to eat the meat roasted over the fire, along with bitter herbs, and bread made without yeast" (Exodus 12:8).

Exodus 12:12–13 gives commentary on the lamb's blood: "On that same night I will pass through Egypt and strike down every firstborn—both men and animals—and I will bring judgment on all the gods of Egypt. I am the LORD. The blood will be a sign for you on the houses where you are; and when I see the blood, I will pass over you. No destructive plague will touch you when I strike Egypt."

Our Savior, God's Son, became the sacrificial lamb. "[Jesus] took the cup saying, 'This cup is the new covenant in my blood: do this, whenever you drink it, in remembrance of Me.' For whenever you eat this bread and drink this cup, you proclaim the Lord's death until He comes" (1 Corinthians 11:25–26).

Who can take the Lord's Supper? Any Christian who has a personal faith that Jesus Christ died for his or her sins may partake. But prior to participating, "A man ought to examine himself before he eats of the bread and drinks of the cup. For anyone who eats and drinks without recognizing the body of the Lord eats and drinks judgment on himself" (1 Corinthians 11:28–29).

Think About It

A father was riding through the country with his son when a bee flew in the window of their car. The son, who was allergic to bee stings, panicked—but then he watched his father catch the bee in his hand, close his hand with a grimace, and open his hand to reveal the lifeless bee. His words to his son remind us of Jesus's broken body and shed blood: "I took the stinger out so you would not have to suffer the pain."

What This Means to You

The Hebrew word *zakar* is sprinkled throughout the Old Testament. *Zakar* means "remember." Every time you partake of the bread and the cup, you obey Jesus's command to remember what your Savior did on your behalf.

Chapter 7
The Four Gospels

Why are there four Gospels rather than one single Gospel that tells the story of Jesus?

What the Bible Has to Say

For prophecy never had its origin in the will of man, but men spoke from God as they were carried along by the Holy Spirit. (2 Peter 1:21)

The word *gospel* is an old one which simply means "good news." It refers explicitly to what Jesus Christ has done to save mankind from the penalty of sin and to provide him the gift of eternal life. The accounts of Jesus's life, which include His ministry, His message, and His role as the Savior who makes our salvation (or new life in Him) possible, are found in the gospels of Matthew, Mark, Luke, and John.

Why are there four Gospels? It is not because four different men who had witnessed the incredible life, death, and resurrection of Jesus decided to each write down their observations; rather, each Gospel was intentionally designed to communicate to a targeted audience with a particular purpose and group of recipients in mind. To put it a different way, the life of Jesus was presented in surround sound to enhance its completeness and to target both Jews and Gentiles (non-Jews). The message reached different groups of people in a more universal audience with a more worldwide appeal. Under the direction of the Holy Spirit, this quartet of men gave us a composite portrait of Jesus.

Matthew, the first Gospel, was primarily written to a Jewish audience. The tax collector turned disciple uses more Old Testament quotes than any other Gospel writer. He does not employ the phrase "kingdom of God," instead, he uses "kingdom of heaven" to avoid offending the Jews. The book opens with a genealogy that links Jesus with King David, the greatest of all the Jewish rulers. His purpose is to convey to his readers that Jesus is the long-awaited *Messiah*. The Messiah was a deliverer predicted by the prophets, who would come to free the Jewish nation from the bondage that stemmed from their failure to obey God's laws and will for their lives.

Mark is the shortest of the four Gospels. It is called the "gospel of immediacy" because he uses some form or synonym of the word "immediately" more than forty times in sixteen chapters. Mark's writings have a Latin flavor in their expression, and it appears his Gospel had particular resonance with Romans. He is painting a picture of Jesus as the servant who came to suffer for our sins. Many Christian teachers recommend new believers start their reading of the Bible with this Gospel because it is concise, moves quickly, and offers a "highlight film" of Jesus.

Luke, the third Gospel, is the only book of the Bible written by a non-Jew. He was a physician who traveled with the apostle Paul. Like a doctor, he is detailed in his descriptions of events. For example, he informs the reader that Peter cut off the right ear of the servant of the high priest when the crowd came to arrest Jesus (Luke 22:50).

Luke's favorite description of Jesus is "Son of Man" which he uses twenty-six times in his Gospel. His Greek, the language the New Testament was written in, is the most refined and sophisticated of any writer in the New Testament. This fact would make his record more appealing to the educated Greeks he targeted with the narrative of Jesus Christ. Also Luke gives us the most in-depth understanding of Jesus's prayer life, including nine of Jesus's prayers, which is more than any other Gospel.

The first three Gospels are labeled *synoptic,* meaning they see (*optic*) and present Jesus in a similar way (*syn*); however, the fourth Gospel, written by *John,* has a different design. John features many "signs" in his writings about Jesus. His purpose is to highlight the deity of Jesus. John spends half of his Gospel on one week of Jesus's life, zooming in on the final week of our Lord's life before His death on the cross and His resurrection from the dead. John's purpose is the broadest and most universal of the Gospels, targeting the whole world. John summarizes his Gospel in John 3:16: "For God so loved the world that He gave His one and only Son, that whoever believes in Him shall not perish but have eternal life."

Think About It

If four men were each standing on a different corner of an intersection when an accident occurred, would not their observations provide a fuller, more holistic account of the event? The Father, Son, and Holy Spirit have granted us four different accounts through four different men so the distribution and reception of the gospel of Jesus Christ would be more impactful upon the inhabitants of Planet Earth. Each of these men—Matthew, Mark, Luke, and John—are part of a beautiful quartet that allows us to hear, understand, and experience the beauty and majesty of our Savior.

What This Means to You

Make sure you read and think about all four Gospels, for this will provide a fuller understanding of who Jesus is and what He has done on your behalf.

Chapter 8
Translations of the Bible

What does the word translation *mean? What is a good translation of the Bible to use in my private study and public worship?*

What the Bible Has to Say

For prophecy never had its origin in the will of man, but men spoke from God as they were carried along by the Holy Spirit. (2 Peter 1:21)

The Bible is a book written by men and inspired by God. Its origins can be traced back to God moving over men through the Holy Spirit. Second Timothy 3:16–17 informs us that "All Scripture is God-breathed and is useful for teaching, rebuking, correcting and training in righteousness, so that the man of God may be thoroughly equipped for every good work." Simply put, the Bible is a divine book. However, since the Bible was written in Hebrew, Aramaic, and Greek, and since most of us don't speak or read those languages, we must purchase a translation.

What is a translation? A Bible translation converts the original language to the English language. It is a crossing over from one language to another. A translation is also called a version. Are there different types of translations? Yes, some translations are *idiomatic*, or "word for word," like the King James Version or The English Standard Version. Others are dynamic, or "phrase by phrase," such as the New International Version. Both approaches are generally acceptable and produce similar results.

There are over fifty English translations that are popular today. You may find this smorgasbord of translations confusing, so I would recommend the following considerations:

1. If the local church you are attending uses a certain translation in public worship, it would seem practical to start with that translation.

2. You may want to seek out a pastor or Christian leader in the church you are attending and ask his or her advice on the decision.

3. You could visit a Christian bookstore and survey the Bibles that are available and also seek counsel from the bookstore staff.

In looking over the many reliable translations that various Christians use with great success, you may see the term *paraphrase* on some Bibles. A paraphrase is a restatement of the original words in English, not a crossover from the original language into English. Therefore, a translation is usually much truer to the original text because it is only one step removed from the original, while a paraphrase is two steps removed from the original.

Why then, you may ask, do new translations keep appearing? Because language changes over time, meaning certain words and phrases do not hold their same meaning, and new words and phrases enter the English vocabulary. In order to be accurate, a new translation is needed to preserve the intended meaning of the text. Sometimes a speaker who has studied Hebrew, Aramaic, or Greek will give additional meaning to a word in the English translation because not all languages have equivalent meanings for the same word. This additional commentary is welcome because it adds augmented understanding to the presentation of God's Word.

Think About It

If you were traveling in Germany, and you did not understand the German language, you might carry a book that translated words from German into English. Or, you may have a personal interpreter with you who would relay the meaning of German words to you in English. This is the value of a Bible translation in your study of God's Word— it is in a language familiar to you and can be easily understood and embraced.

What This Means to You

Be thankful that men and women have spent years developing an accurate translation. If you don't have a Bible translation or version, follow the three steps suggested in securing one.

Chapter 9
Studying the Bible

How do I study the Word of God in a productive manner?

What the Bible Has to Say

Study to shew thyself approved unto God, a workman that needeth not to be ashamed, rightly dividing the Word of truth. (2 Timothy 2:15 KJV)

When you study the Bible, you find yourself face-to-face with the thoughts of God. You have the edge in life because you are the beneficiary of God's wisdom and counsel. Second Timothy 3:16-17 provides a list of the benefits of studying the Scriptures: "All Scripture is God-breathed and is useful for teaching, rebuking, correcting and training in righteousness, so that the man of God may be thoroughly equipped for every good work."

How do we study the Bible to harvest maximum value from its pages? Many of those who teach and write on this subject have followed a three-step approach that can be used with every book of the Bible, despite the diversity of authorship, subject material, and time of writing. These steps are *observation*, *interpretation*, and *application*:

1. *Observation* leads us to ask the question, "What does it say?" The student is harvesting from the Scripture the simple truths from the text of the Bible. This is different from reading into the text our preconceived thoughts and the thoughts of others. We simply and methodically make notes on the basic words and ideas that are found in the straightforward reading of a Bible passage.

2. *Interpretation* points us to the question, "What does it mean?" This step often necessitates us asking who was the author, who was his target audience, and what was his primary purpose. We may need to study some of the key words so we can fully understand the significance of a passage. Finally, we may need to ask what prevailing problem or challenge the author and the believers were facing in that day and time.

3. *Application* brings us to the question, "What does it mean for my life?" This step is often neglected or devalued. The Bible's truths were written for your salvation and spiritual success. They are designed to be a manual for living. This third step leads to changing our habits and priorities, our responses and reactions. The application of the truth is what prompts us to live a more influential and powerful life for the Lord.

Let's consider a verse and engage it with these three steps in mind. First John 1:9 states, "If we confess our sins, He is faithful and just and will forgive us our sins and purify us from all unrighteousness." Without trying to be exhaustive, we might come to some of these conclusions:

Observations:

- The word *if* is used indicating the idea is conditional.

- Confession is a part of the disciple's experience.

- Confession is necessary because of sin.

- Confession is made to a God who is faithful to forgive.

- God's forgiveness is absolute, for it refers to "all unrighteousness."

Interpretation:

- The author, John, was writing to believers (1 John 2:12–14; 3:1; 5:13).

- Some believers were claiming they did not sin (1 John 1:8, 10).

- The word *confess* means "to say the same thing," therefore two parties are involved.

- The two parties are the Holy Spirit, who tells us we have violated God's law, and the one who has sinned, who agrees with the Holy Spirit that a sin has been committed.

- The word for sin means "to miss the mark," like an archer whose arrow falls short of the target.

- Our confession results in the removal of impurities and the restoration of a right relationship with our Lord.

Application:

- As a believer, you must be aware you will sin.

- When you sin, you should keep short accounts and agree with the Holy Spirit who has revealed this failure to you.

- You should emerge from this confession knowing God has removed the contaminants from your soul, giving you confidence and new hope.

Think About It

A Boy Scout uses a compass to find and follow the right direction to his intended destination. However, if he doesn't consult the compass or doesn't understand how to use it, the value of this important instrument is diminished. God's Word, the Bible, is the primary directional tool in the believer's backpack. We need to consult the Bible and properly study it, so it has the maximum navigational value in our lives. If we follow the three steps of basic Bible study, we will harvest a great deal from God's Book.

What This Means to You

The reading of the Bible has value, but the study of the Bible will result in even more profit to your life of faith. Read God's Word, but also take time to study and meditate on its truth and discern how that truth can be applied to your life.

Chapter 10
Daily Devotions

How critical is it that I spend daily time with God in prayer and studying His Word?

What the Bible Has to Say

Jesus answered, "It is written: 'Man does not live on bread alone, but on every Word that comes from the mouth of God.'" (Matthew 4:4)

Our daily time with God, often called "daily devotions" or "daily bread," has a significant role on our health, or lack thereof, as we seek to walk and live like Jesus. Jesus went regularly to a solitary place to pray (Matthew 14:23), and in the theme verse, Jesus describes God's Word as necessary to living.

As the disciple begins each day of service to God, there should be a time of devotions and prayer to lubricate the mind and soul for the challenges ahead. These daily briefings with God allow us to navigate the map He provides for each day of our lives. Without them we start to run into heart trouble, we lose our way, we slow down, and sometimes we end up in a life accident. The Creator has designed us to feed on His Word regularly and systematically. God's Word is nutrition, life-food to the believer. In other words, "It is daily bread—or daily dead."

How do most of us begin our days? Most humans wash up, get dressed, and eat a morning meal. Our devotional life facilitates these same actions in a spiritual context. Ephesians 5:26 describes the church as being "washed by the water of the Word." When Paul spoke of the spiritual wardrobe in Ephesians 6, he likened the Word of God to a "belt of truth" and the "sword of the Spirit." What happens when we forget our belt or a warrior reaches for his sword and the sheath is empty?

Psalm 119 is relevant to the daily devotions discussion. It is divided into twenty-two, eight-verse segments, one segment for each of the twenty-two letters of the Hebrew alphabet. This acrostic Scripture passage provides a clinic on the strategic nature of God's Word. How does a young man keep pure? The answer is profoundly simple: Live by God's Word (Psalm 119:9). How do we keep from sinning? The psalmist writes in 119:11, "I have hidden your Word in my heart that I might not sin against you." The Word of God is a guiding light for our Christian walk: "Your Word is a lamp to my feet and a light for my path" (Psalm 119:105).

As a pastor for almost four decades, I have counseled hundreds of people. I can assure you when a person's devotional life has dried up, he or she is a candidate for a tragic sin or failure. *There is basically a one-to-one correlation between no devotions and anemic Christianity.*

It is imperative that we place daily time with God on our schedules. If we miss that appointment, all other appointments have less significance. "In the morning, my prayer comes before you" (Psalm 88:13). If not, in the evening you and I will count the defeats of our daily living. I have written in my Bible this sobering truth: "Sin will keep me from this book, or this book will keep me from sin!"

Think About It

I enjoy collectibles. My love for history draws me like a magnet to old baseball cards, old coins, and old furniture. My brother enjoys old relics too, but due to his taste and bankbook, he can shop at much more expensive stores. One Thanksgiving he took me to his downstairs garage and showed me the 1930 Packard he had jointly purchased with a friend for $25,000. Denny gave us an introduction to this magnificently maintained automobile. The shiny chrome fenders, leather seats, and old-fashioned steering wheel captured my attention. However, one feature intrigued me more than any other: the auto lube lever. A pencil-thin conduit for lubrication was woven throughout this car, and every day the driver was supposed to pull this lever; oil would ooze its way into the vehicle, so it was capable of travel. No pull on the lever, no preparation for the journey. We need to pull the "daily devotions lever" every day.

What This Means to You

A daily time with God needs to be on your schedule. It is your daily bread that gives you the potential to live a vigorous and vital life like Jesus. Without this time, you will find yourself hurtling headlong toward malnutrition and defeat. This is a meal you cannot afford to miss.

Chapter 11
Leading Someone to Jesus

How do I lead my friends to Jesus? How do I show the way to those who hear my story and then desire to become followers of Jesus Christ?

What the Bible Has to Say

That if you confess with your mouth, "Jesus is Lord," and believe in your heart that God raised Him from the dead, you will be saved. For it is with your heart that you believe and are justified, and it is with your mouth that you confess and are saved. (Romans 10:9–10)

When you accepted Jesus Christ as Lord and Savior, you probably were filled with great joy and new hope for your life on earth and your eternal life in heaven. As your family and friends noticed a difference in your life and you told them your story of finding Jesus, perhaps many of them were stirred in their hearts to hear more about your transformation.

As you told them, the Holy Spirit may have drawn them to a point of decision, and they reached out to you (or will in the near future) to also receive Jesus. Your faith became contagious. Now what do you say or do to lead them through the process of conversion (becoming a believer in Christ) and help them realign their lives with the life and love of Jesus?

When I was in my twenties, I served on the staff of an evangelistic organization. I was taught the "Roman Road"—a series of verses from the New Testament book of Romans—as a pathway to lead a person to Jesus. Decades have passed, and this method is still effective and relevant. The steps on the "Roman Road" are as follows:

- Romans 3:23: "For all have sinned and fall short of the glory of God." —Admit that you are a sinner and need a Savior.

- Romans 6:23a: "The wages of sin is death," —Understand that sin pays and the payment is death.

- Romans 6:23b: "but the gift of God is eternal life in Christ Jesus our Lord." —Salvation is a free gift from God to you. You can't earn this gift; you must receive it.

- Romans 5:8: "But God demonstrates His own love for us in this: While we were still sinners Christ died for us." —God loved you first. Now give your life to God. His love, demonstrated by Jesus's death on the cross, is your only effective hope for forgiveness and new life.

- Romans 14:12: "So then, each of us will give an account of himself to God." —Who will give an account to God? Everyone! No one is exempt.

- Romans 10:13: "Everyone who calls on the name of the Lord will be saved." —Call out to God in the name of Jesus.

- Romans 10:9–10: "That if you confess with your mouth, 'Jesus is Lord,' and believe in your heart that God raised Him from the dead, you will be saved. For it is with your heart that you believe and are justified, and it is with your mouth that you confess and are saved." —As you tell the Lord you need Him, and as you believe in the resurrection of Jesus, you are forgiven and granted a new beginning as a member of God's family.

Now tell your story to someone else.

Think About It

If your doctor discovered the cure for a chronic disease such as diabetes, and you were given the medicine, which worked, would you be reluctant to tell your family and friends (who suffer with this same malady)? No, you would be a public relations powerhouse, sharing the good news that a cure had been found. This is how it should be when you discover that you can be forgiven and be part of God's family, both here and forevermore.

What This Means to You

When someone asks you for a pathway to salvation in Jesus Christ, you can share with them the "Roman Road."

Chapter 12
Obedience

What value does the Lord put on my obedience to His commands?
What are the positive and negative consequences of my obedience?

What the Bible Has to Say

Does the Lord delight in burnt offerings and sacrifices as much as in obeying the voice of the Lord? To obey is better than sacrifice, and to heed than the fat of rams. (1 Samuel 15:22)

This Scripture reveals the value God puts on obedience. The king of Israel, Saul, was commanded to attack the Amalekites and totally destroy everything belonging to them (1 Samuel 15:3). Saul did attack the Amalekites; however, the text tells us: "Saul and the army spared Agag (the king of the Amalekites) and the best of the sheep and cattle, the fat calves and lambs—everything that was good (15:9). The command of God had been compromised. When Samuel confronted Saul with his disobedience, Saul argued that the best sheep and cattle were preserved to be sacrificed to God in worship.

"To obey is better than to sacrifice," was Samuel's assessment, and the historic consequence was "He [God] has rejected you [Saul] as king"

(15:23). Even the idea of worship did not overrule the commandment of the Lord, and consequently, a king lost his throne.

In my study of the Bible for over fifty years, I have come to this conclusion: *obedience* may be the most important word in the Bible. I offer this opinion because obedience is so closely intertwined with such important words as faith and love. For example, obedience and faith cannot be divorced in God's Word. In John 8:31 Jesus spoke to Jews who had believed in Him and issued this qualifier, "If you hold to My teaching [obey it] you are really My disciples." Obedience is a characteristic of discipleship, true faith, and belief.

In the opening verses of the book of Romans, Paul unfolds God's purpose for him "to call people from among all the Gentiles to the obedience that comes from faith" (Romans 1:5). In the closing verses of Romans, Paul returns to this same theme, instructing his readers that the proclamation of the gospel and the writings of the prophets are "by the command of the eternal God, so that all nations might believe and obey Him" (16:26). The Lord's expectation is that believers obey His commands and instructions.

Obedience is also inextricably linked and coupled with love. Jesus taught His disciples this on the eve of His arrest and crucifixion, as He sought to prepare them for these climactic events. In John 14:15, He makes this defining statement: "If you love me, you will obey what I command." Love cannot be separated from obedience. Later He adds, "If you obey My commands, you will remain in My love, just as I have obeyed My Father's commands and remain in His love" (John 15:10). We realize again the weight God places on obedience and how it is connected to God's love and the correlation of Jesus obeying His Father and the love the Father bestows on Him.

Obedience plays a huge role in determining our identity and destiny. In Exodus 19:5, Moses was directed by the Lord to speak to the people of Israel these strategic words: "Now if you obey me fully and keep My covenant, then out of all the nations, you will be My treasured possession."

In Deuteronomy 28, we discover a continental divide that was presented to the Jewish people. The chapter lays out the blessings for obedience and the curses for disobedience. Consider Deuteronomy 28:1-2 as the chapter opens, "If you fully obey the Lord your God and carefully follow all His commands I give you today, the Lord God will set you high above the nations on earth. All these blessings will come upon you and accompany you if you obey the Lord your God."

Consider the counterpoint in Deuteronomy 28:15: "However, if you do not obey the Lord your God and do not carefully follow all His commands and decrees I am giving you today, all these curses will come upon you and overtake you."

Obedience is serious business with the Lord. Don't take it lightly, for He honors those who obey Him, but He punishes those who disobey and rebel against Him. If you go against the grain of God's universe, you are going to get splinters.

Think About It

Near the end of the Sermon on the Mount (Matthew 5-7), Jesus warns His listeners that saying, "Jesus is Lord of my life," is not enough: "Not everyone who says to me, 'Lord, Lord,' will enter the kingdom of heaven, but only he who does the will of my Father in heaven" (Matthew 7:21).

It is not enough to talk the talk; you and I must walk the walk.

What This Means to You

You may think you have a better idea, a more profitable path, a more correct decision, but the Lord declares, "So are my ways higher than your ways and My thoughts than your thoughts" (Isaiah 55:9).

He wrote the playbook, so run His plays and obey His ways.

Chapter 13
Temptation

How do I cope successfully with temptation?

What the Bible Has to Say

No temptation has seized you except what is common to man. And God is faithful; He will not let you be tempted beyond what you can bear. But when you are tempted, He will also provide a way out so that you can stand up under it. (1 Corinthians 10:13)

Temptations are enticements designed to trick you into breaking commandments, to lure you into disobeying God, and to cause you to fall short of the Lord's expectations for you. Everyone is tempted—even Jesus was tempted.

The theme verse from 1 Corinthians is one of the most helpful in the Bible. First, it tells you that none of the temptations that come before you are unique. They have been experienced by others before you. Secondly, God is faithful, and He has promised not to allow you to experience a temptation you cannot defeat. In other words, He limits our temptations so we can bear them and overcome them. Thirdly, when temptations come, you are not boxed in with no way of escape; the Lord always provides a door or window as an escape route. The phrase "a way out" in the original language means "to be surrounded by an army, with an escape route available." If we are willing to escape, there will be a way of escape.

As the Lord Jesus taught His disciples to pray, His model prayer included this petition: "And lead us not into temptation, but deliver us from the evil one" (Matthew 6:13; see also the shorter version in Luke 11:4). We can be confident that God is not the tempter. James made this clear in his letter: "When tempted, no one should say, 'God is tempting me.' For God cannot be tempted by evil, nor does He tempt anyone; but each one is tempted when, by his own evil desire, he is dragged away and enticed" (James 1:13–14). When Jesus was agonizing over His impending death in the garden of Gethsemane, He instructed His disciples to "Sit here while I pray" (Mark 14:32). However, when He came back to them, He found them sleeping. Jesus gave them some sound advice which is pertinent to every believer, "Watch and pray so that you will not fall into temptation. The spirit is willing but the body is weak" (Mark 14:38).

We know His disciples disregarded His counsel because He found them sleeping two other times during this significant night of prayer. Peter also gave some warning words: "Be self-controlled and alert. Your enemy the devil prowls around like a roaring lion looking for someone to devour" (1 Peter 5:8). The enemy is salivating to take a bite out of your life—no, not just a bite; he wants to completely devour you.

As you attempt to successfully deal with temptations, you also can observe and apply the principles of Jesus when He was tempted by the devil. This account is found in Matthew 4:1–11, Luke 4:1–13, and is briefly mentioned in Mark 1:12–13. Jesus had fasted forty days and nights after being led by the Holy Spirit into the wilderness. The devil tempted Him three times. The devil even quoted Old Testament Scriptures to lead the Savior astray. Each time, Jesus responded with Scriptures from Deuteronomy to counteract Satan's plan. It is beneficial to note that He endured these temptations by fasting and praying, and His most powerful weapon was the Word of God. In Hebrews 4:15 we read, "For we do not have a high priest who is unable to sympathize without weaknesses, but we have one who has been tempted in every way, just as we are—yet was without sin."

We are not perfect like Jesus Christ, but we can be certain He understands what we are going through. We can practice some of the principles He utilized in His victories over temptation. And we can be confident God limits our temptations and always provides a pathway out of them.

Think About It

I remember one of my pastors telling the story of a lady who came to a prayer meeting and offered this testimony: "I am so thankful I am never tempted."

His response was, "If you are never tempted, then Satan must already have you."

You cannot escape being tempted, but you can escape any and all temptations.

What This Means to You

Temptations are like death and taxes—you cannot avoid them. Be alert, be prayerful, deploy Scripture, and walk or climb through the door or window God will provide for your escape.

Chapter 14
Suffering Because of Sin

Is all suffering due to sins that have been committed?

What the Bible Has to Say

As He [Jesus] went along, He saw a blind man from birth. His disciples asked him, "Rabbi, who sinned, this man or his parents, that he was born blind?" "Neither this man nor his parents sinned," said Jesus, "but this happened so that the work of God might be displayed in his life." (John 9:1-3)

The Bible is clear that sometimes our sins are the reasons for our suffering. Psalm 107:17–18 is explicit about this cause and effect relationship: "Some became fools through their rebellious ways and suffered affliction because of their iniquities. They loathed all food and drew near to the gates of death." Paul even went further by asserting in Romans 6:23, "For the wages of sin is death." Sin has consequences. However, sometimes God uses those painful consequences to turn someone toward Him.

If we look further into Psalm 107:19–20, we discover that affliction became a tool in God's hands: "Then they cried to the Lord in their trouble, and He saved them from their distress. He sent forth His word and healed them; He rescued them from the grave." Suffering and afflictions can become wake-up calls to draw us to change our attitudes and lifestyles, to turn from waywardness to worship.

However, not all suffering has a direct connection to sin. John 9 tells the story of the man blind from birth. The disciples' knee-jerk response to encountering the blind man was, "Who sinned, this man or his parents, that he was born blind?" Jesus countered that neither the man nor his parents had prompted this malady; instead, the blindness would serve as an opportunity "that the work of God might be displayed in his life." God the Father had allowed the blindness so Jesus the Son would heal him; this sparked the man to arrive at a place where he could say, "Lord, I believe," and he worshiped Jesus (John 9:38).

When Paul was saying goodbye to the church leaders in Ephesus, he reminded them that his future sufferings would be used by the Lord to forward his ministry of declaring God's truth in various venues. Paul confided in these leaders, "And now, compelled by the Spirit, I am going to Jerusalem, not knowing what will happen to me there. I only know that in every city the Holy Spirit warns me that prison and hardships are facing me. However, I consider my life worth nothing to me; my only aim is to finish the race and complete the task the Lord Jesus has given me—the task of testifying to the good news of God's grace" (Acts 20:22–24). His purpose and God's plan were wrapped up in the circumstances of suffering, not because of Paul's sin but rather to accomplish God's plan.

The story of Job, in the Old Testament, provides evidence that suffering can sometimes brutally assault a man, not because he has sinned (as Job's friends argued), but because he is blameless. Fortunately, Job persevered in his faith, trusting that God was just and was working through his pain.

Think About It

Dietrich Bonhoeffer died in a Nazi concentration camp because he tried to save Jews from the Holocaust. He was not guilty of any sin, but his life was still terminated. He wrote this about being a follower of Jesus: "Suffering, then, is the true badge of discipleship. The disciple is not above his master. Following Christ means *passio passiva*, suffering because we have to suffer."

What This Means to You

Don't be too hasty to judge the suffering of others or yourself. Sometimes the affliction is a vital part of God's plan to display His glory. The cross of Jesus Christ is a powerful example of the suffering of an innocent person to accomplish a great outcome for God and His people.

Chapter 15
Confession

What is the meaning of confession?
What bearing does it have on the health of my Christian life?

What the Bible Has to Say

If we confess our sins, He is faithful and just and will forgive us our sins and purify us from all unrighteousness. (1 John 1:9)

Confession is an integral part of our Christian experience. When we come to Jesus we are initially forgiven of all our sins, but that does not preclude our sinning in the future. Even after becoming followers of Jesus Christ, we will still fall short of God's will and break His commandments.

In the physical realm, if a person is healed from a serious infection, it does not mean he or she will never acquire an infection again. Fortunately, the same medicine that treated the first infection will usually treat the second one as well. Likewise, in the spiritual realm, from time to time we will commit new sins, and they can be dealt with by confessing them to the Lord as we did when we first came to Christ. His gracious response is to purify us and make us completely whole in our soul again.

Even after the early disciples were filled with the Holy Spirit at the great Jewish festival called Pentecost (Acts 2), that did not prevent them from still sinning. An excellent example is found in Galatians 2:11–13 when Paul confronted Peter with the fact that he was clearly in the wrong. Peter had been eating and fellowshipping with the Gentiles (non-Jews), but when his Jewish friends came along, he separated himself from the Gentile converts, even though they had been brought into God's family. Paul's words were stark: Peter and the other Jews were "not acting in line with the truth of the gospel" (Galatians 2:14)—in other words, they were sinning. Indeed, it must be true that believers can sin and need forgiveness because the theme verse (1 John 1:9) is from a book written to believers.

The word confession comes from two Greek words, *homo*, which means the same, and *logos*, which means word or speech. Literally, the word means, "to say the same thing." Who are the two persons saying the same thing? They are the Holy Spirit and the one who has sinned. Here's an example of how confession might take place. For instance, suppose I said something hurtful and unkind to my wife, Faye. The Holy Spirit might speak to me and say, "Arnie, you should not have spoken in such an insensitive and mean way."

I should agree with the Spirit by saying, "You are so right, Lord. I am sorry for how I spoke to Faye, and I ask You to forgive me for my sinful speech and the motives behind it."

Both of us agreed; we said the same thing about my speech. That is how confession works in the Christian context. According to *The New International Dictionary of the New Testament*, the one who confesses his or her sin acknowledges it and does not try to hide nor deny it (Vol. 1, p. 346).

Confession is a healthy discipline of the disciple who follows Jesus. If one tries to hide and conceal sin, it results in prolonged guilt and soaks up tremendous energy which could have been invested in fruitful ministry and service. When David wrote Psalm 32, a penitential psalm, he cataloged the physical and spiritual liabilities of trying to conceal sin. He penned these words: "When I kept silent, my bones wasted away" (v. 3), but later in the psalm, he wrote, "Then I acknowledged my sin to You and did not cover up my iniquity. I said, 'I will confess my transgressions to the Lord'—and You forgave the guilt of my sin" (v. 5).

David went from uptight to upright and ended the psalm with rejoicing. So it is when we confess: God's heavy hand on our lives when we tolerate unconfessed sin is replaced by God's healing hand on our hearts when we access His incredible mercy and grace.

Think About It

In the epic *Star Trek* series, the Klingons used stealth technology to render their starships invisible, and it worked well. The only problem was that the energy used to cloak the ship was diverted from the ship's weapons; whenever a Klingon ship was cloaked, it had no power to effectively attack. If we expend our energy trying to hide our sins (in a sense, to *cloak* them), we will not possess the energy to serve the Lord wholeheartedly and live a powerful Christian life.

What This Means to You

Confession is a normal and healthy component of Christian living. The Lord has provided this means of dealing with your failures and sins in order that you may have short accounts of debt and long litanies of effective and noble Christian ministry.

Chapter 16
Discipline

*What is the role of discipline in a believer's life and
what benefits are harvested from it?*

What the Bible Has to Say

*My son, do not make light of the Lord's discipline, and do not lose heart
when He rebukes you, because the Lord disciplines those He loves, and
He punishes everyone He accepts as a son.* (Hebrews 12:5–6)

Disciple and *discipline* come from the same root word. The word
disciple is certainly more appealing; it means a learner, pupil, or
student. When you accepted Jesus Christ as Lord and Savior, you were
called to be His disciple. However, to be a disciple will mean discipline
has to be administered at times. The word points to teaching or
training that entails correction, pain, or suffering. You probably relish
the thought of being labeled a disciple, but you don't look forward to
the discipline that is necessary to develop a mature disciple.

The Hebrews 12:5–6 theme verse instructs us not to underestimate
the value of the Lord's discipline. It goes on to say that there is the
possibility of losing heart when we are rebuked by the Lord. Rebuke
can be defined as confronting a person with the consequences of their

choices. When the rebuke takes place, it points to a failure, an action that was in bad taste, or sometimes even a sinful act. This is not the place we want to be, but the purpose of the Lord is not to discourage us, but to remind us that the Lord's motivation is *love*, and His purpose is to make us a more successful son or daughter in His kingdom family.

My wrestling coach in high school was not hard on us in practice. Often, he didn't push us to expend ourselves. We enjoyed his easy-going demeanor, which translated into less-than-challenging practices. However, when we wrestled in the official match, we often regretted that he had not disciplined us and developed us by extra training and Spartan exercises. The discipline of the Lord is not just punitive; it is developmental and results in a more "muscular" follower of Jesus Christ, whose weaknesses have been corrected and whose strengths present more opportunity for success and victory. The pruning of a plant may seem harmful to a child, but to one who understands horticulture and has seen the benefits of reshaping the plant and redirecting its energies, it is a positive procedure.

The New Testament is clear that sometimes a church member must be disciplined. There are many actions that may call for church discipline, such as causing divisions (Romans 16:17), sexual immorality (1 Corinthians 5:1–13), causing grief in another person (2 Corinthians 2:5–8), and wandering from the truth (James 5:19–20). If there is no repentance, and there is repeated failure and persistent resistance to change, it could lead to expulsion. But the Bible also speaks of reaffirming our love for the offender (2 Corinthians 2:8) and in the process of restoration covering a multitude of sins (James 5:19–20). Hebrews again sheds a bright light on the constructive side of discipline: "God disciplines us for our good that we may share in holiness. No discipline seems pleasant at the time, but painful. However, later on it produces a harvest of righteousness and peace for those who have been trained by it" (Hebrews 12:10–11).

Think About It

I remember my mother saying, before she disciplined me for some wayward action, "This hurts me more than it hurts you."

In my carnal little mind, I thought, "Then spank yourself!" Looking back, I understand the spanking was motivated by a love for me and was driven by a vision to prevent me from making the same mistake again. Tough love leads to triumphant disciples.

What This Means to You

Discipline is included in the meal that is served to a disciple. A lack of discipline will limit the health and holiness of a follower of Jesus Christ. The popular sentiment, "Without pains, no gains," dates from the 1500s (Ammer, 2003), and this is true for your Christian walk.

Chapter 17
Faith

How does the Bible define faith and what role
does it play in my Christian life?

What the Bible Has to Say

Now faith is being sure of what we hope for and certain of what we do
not see. (Hebrews 11:1)

When I was at seminary, my independent master's project was to study the word *faith* in the New Testament. There are over 550 occurrences of this word in its noun, adjective, and verb forms. After all this time and effort, I came up with a rather long, but I believe complete, definition of faith: "Faith is the fully confident attitude and inevitably obedient action in response to the demands of God, who has exhibited His trustworthiness, for a complete consecration of self and possessions." In a much shorter definition, we can describe faith as "belief in, trust in, and dependence on someone or something."

Faith is an investment of ourselves in a belief that an event will definitely occur before we have all the evidence to prove it will happen. Faith believes before we actually see something in reality. How important is faith? Hebrews 11:6 gives a concise answer to this question: "And without faith it is impossible to please God, because anyone who comes to Him must believe that He exists and that He rewards those that diligently seek him." Faith is a nonnegotiable component of the Christian's life.

You may hear the expression "saving faith." This pertains to our initial salvation experience through our belief and trust in Jesus Christ. John 3:16 highlights the necessity of belief: "For God so loved the world that He gave His one and only Son, that whoever believes in Him shall not perish but have eternal life." Believing Jesus died on the cross for our sins and trusting He paid the penalty that we should have paid for our moral failures is sufficient to secure our salvation and procure eternal and everlasting life. We then experience what many term "the assurance of salvation," and we live differently after this faith commitment because we are now following Jesus. In the book of Acts, we discover the plea of the Philippian jailer who, following an earthquake, appealed to Paul and Silas, "Sirs, what must I do to be saved?" (Acts 16:30). Their reply was swift and decisive: "Believe in the Lord Jesus, and you will be saved" (v.31).

When you invested your faith in Jesus, you inserted the key into the door that opened the way of salvation. Paul provides a two-part equation for our salvation to enter into relationship with Jesus in Romans 10:9-10: "That if you confess with your mouth, Jesus is Lord, and believe in your heart that God raised Him from the dead, you will be saved. For it is with your heart that you believe and are justified, and it is with your mouth that you confess and are saved." Again, the imperative of faith is present in the process of God saving us and liberating us from our sins and the consequences that emerge from them.

The Bible is clear that faith leads to actions such as obedience and service. If we truly believe in God, our lives will be marked by acts which flow out from our faith. The most prominent verses that point us toward this spiritual reality are found in James 2:14–17: "What good is it, my brothers, if a man claims to have faith, but has no deeds? Can such faith save him? Suppose a brother or sister is without clothes and daily food. If one of you says to him, 'Go, I wish you well; keep warm and well fed,' but does nothing about his physical needs, what good is it? In the same way, faith by itself, if it is not accompanied by action, is dead. But someone will say, 'You have faith; I have deeds. Show me your faith without deeds, and I will show you my faith by what I do.'"

True, authentic faith will result in good deeds and works of service.

Think About It

Everyone on the planet exhibits faith every day. For example, each time you open a can of soup, you demonstrate faith in, trust in, and dependence on those who created and developed the product. You did not witness the selection of the ingredients; you did not verify the product being poured into the can. Yet you still believe you can open, heat, and eat the can of soup. You have demonstrated faith in the process and the persons who produced the can of soup.

What This Means to You

Faith is necessary to find salvation in Jesus, to obey the commands of God's Word, and to produce works of service. Your faith is a well-placed investment if it is placed in the Lord, His Word, and the reality of His kingdom.

Chapter 18
Hope

What is Christian hope and how does it differ from an unbeliever's hope?

What the Bible Has to Say

Therefore, prepare your minds for action; be self-controlled; set your hope fully on the grace to be given you when Jesus Christ is revealed. (1 Peter 1:13)

In Walt Disney's 1940 adaptation of *Pinocchio*, Jiminy Cricket sang of wishing upon a star for your heart's desires. This wishful thinking does not compare to the hope described in the Bible. Biblical hope is confident and full of expectations rooted in the character of God and the unblemished record of His predictions and promises.

The Bible portrays an eroding world. The media is quick to point out the brokenness of peace between nations, the escalation of conflicts, the pollution of the environment, and the ever-expanding frequency of natural disasters. Nevertheless, the Christian is called to display rock-solid hope in a positive future, as promised in the Holy Scriptures. Not only is the follower of Jesus to believe there is a heaven, but also to see hope in present circumstances. "We know that in all things God works for the good of those who love Him, who have been called according to His purpose" (Romans 8:28). Paul does not say a few circumstances or some circumstances, but all circumstances. Biblical hope results in a lifestyle that is commanded to "be joyful always; pray continually" and "give thanks in all circumstances, for this is God's will for you in Christ Jesus" (1 Thessalonians 5:16–18).

God is described in Paul's prayer in Romans 15:13 as "the God of hope," meaning He alone is the source of true hope for His children. And as we place our trust in Him, not in our synthetic hopes manufactured by pipe dreams and unfounded optimism, Paul's conclusion to his prayer describes us as people who "overflow with hope by the power of the Holy Spirit."

Three adjectives are employed in the New Testament to describe hope: *good* hope in 2 Thessalonians 2:16; *blessed* hope in Titus 2:13; and *living* hope in 1 Peter 1:3. Hope is a strategic component in the arsenal of the disciple of Jesus Christ. Because our hope is anchored in who God is and what He has accomplished through His Son, our hope is resilient. Even in an unraveling society, we remain stable and secure. Even when death strikes our loved ones, we do not "grieve like the rest of men, who have no hope" (1 Thessalonians 4:13). We do not avoid grief, but neither do we surrender to it because we look forward to the promises of the Lord for our resurrection (1 Corinthians 15).

Edward Mote (1797-1874), a cabinetmaker in a London suburb, came to Jesus Christ through the witness of his mentor. His hymn, "My Hope is Built," reflects this biblical hope that embraces the Christian's life. The opening stanza and chorus read:

My hope is built on nothing less
than Jesus' blood and righteousness;
I dare not trust the sweetest frame,
but wholly lean on Jesus' name.
On Christ, the solid rock I stand;
All other ground is sinking sand,
All other ground is sinking sand.

Think About It

Because you have Jesus, you have endless hope; those who don't have Jesus have a hopeless end.

What This Means to You

Where you place your hope will determine your attitude and your altitude. Jesus Christ is the best place to invest your hope, and if you bank on Him, you will not be disappointed.

Chapter 19
Love

How does the Bible define love? What does it look like?

What the Bible Has to Say

For God so loved the world that He gave His one and only Son, that whoever believes in Him should not perish but have eternal life. (John 3:16)

John 3:16 may be the most memorized and quoted verse in the Bible. Its central theme is God's love, which is demonstrated by the offering of His Son, Jesus Christ, to save us from our sins and to give us eternal, everlasting, forever life.

Someone defined love in these practical terms: "Love is making your problem my problem." Although this definition is not all-encompassing, it certainly pertains to John 3:16 and what God did to rescue us from ourselves, our sins, and our destiny, which was to perish. John 3:16 might be paraphrased: "The greatest person (God) loved the greatest object (the world) and gave the greatest gift (His Son) to prevent the greatest punishment (perish) and accomplish the greatest destiny (eternal life)."

The Greeks had three words for love, while in English we have only one. An explanation of these three Greek words may expand our understanding of this strategic word. The lowest level of love was expressed with the word *eros*. This word is the basis for our English word, *erotic*, and is a glandular love. In other words, I love you because you satisfy my physical needs. It is the love expressed by animals—an indiscriminate intimacy, driven by a selfish need to quell physical passions. This word does not appear in the Bible.

The second word, *phileo*, which does appear in the Bible (such as in the name Philadelphia), means "brotherly love"—a more reciprocal relationship: you do something kind to me, and I will do something kind to you.

However, this word falls short of the third word, *agape*, which is unconditional love. Agape is a love with no conditions and no cancellation policy. It is the love expressed by God, and the type of love God expects His children to manifest in their lives—toward Him, toward other believers, toward the world, and toward ourselves. This is no fickle thing, but a firm and resolute love which is not based on the actions or reactions of others.

Romans 5:8 communicates to us, "But God demonstrates His own love for us in this: While we were still sinners, Christ died for us." In other words, God didn't wait until we were perfect or pure to love us, He loved us when we were rebels and disobedient. This unconditional love is the love two people pledge to each other when they are married. *Agape* love is embodied in vows that permit no conditions or considerations to end it. We tell our spouse that our love (*agape*) is "for better or worse, for richer or poorer, in sickness and in health, to love and to cherish, till death do us part." You see, God's love for you is not built on your life; it is rooted and grounded in His unconditional commitment to you, even when you were a sinner—and even now when you sin as a believer.

You will find this love woven throughout the entire Bible. Genesis through Revelation depicts God's agape love toward a fallen humanity. It is also imperative to understand that God expects you and me to display this love to our fellow brothers and sisters. First John 4:11-12 lays down this noble standard: "Dear friends, since God so loved us, we also ought to love one another. No one has ever seen God; but if we love one another, God lives in us and His love is made complete in us." John writes later in the chapter that loving each other is the litmus test for whether we really love God: "If anyone says, 'I love God,' yet hates his brother, he is a liar. For anyone who does not love his brother, whom he has seen, cannot love God, whom he has not seen" (1 John 4:20).

First Corinthians 13 is often called the "Love Chapter." In beautiful and eloquent terms, it portrays agape love at its finest. Other love chapters include Romans 12, 1 John 3, and 1 John 4. These chapters will enlighten and inspire you to portray and pursue love that reaches the highest levels.

Think About It

When asked which commandment in the law was the greatest, our Savior replied, "'Love the Lord your God with all your heart and with all your soul and with all your mind.' This is the first and greatest commandment. And the second is like it: 'Love your neighbor as yourself'" (Matthew 22:37–39). The apostle Paul also added, "Love is the fulfillment of the law" (Romans 13:10).

What This Means to You

Remember God's love is agape—it has no conditions—and as a believer, you are the recipient of this incredible gift. His love is not based on your performance, so when you sin, come to Him, and His gracious forgiveness will cascade over your life. This love was paid for by the sacrifice of Jesus Christ (1 John 4:10).

Hymn writer Frederick Lehman framed God's love in these terms: "The love of God is greater far, than tongue or pen could ever tell; it goes beyond the highest star, and reaches to the lowest hell. The guilty pair, bowed down with care, God gave His Son to win; His erring child He reconciled, and pardoned from his sin." Praise the Lord for His matchless love.

Chapter 20
Fellowship

What does fellowship mean and how critical is it to the life of a believer?

What the Bible Has to Say

They devoted themselves to the apostles' teaching and to the fellowship, to the breaking of bread and to prayer. (Acts 2:42)

The word fellowship is used forty-three times in the New Testament and comes from a root word, *koine,* which means "common." The language of the New Testament is not classical Greek, which is a more elegant and flowery variety; rather, it is *koine* Greek, which is the Greek of the marketplace or "street Greek," a more common dialect spoken by everyone. God purposed that everyone would have the story of Jesus, His teachings, and the writings of the apostles about these issues, in a form accessible to them. The word for fellowship is *koinonia,* and it indicates a common bond that occurs between believers in life and faith. In other words, we are to share our faith and faith walk in Jesus Christ with many people.

The "Lone Ranger," solitary, "alone in the woods with the squirrels" mentality is not the norm for healthy followers of Jesus. It is noteworthy that the only time God stated His creation was not good pertained to the absence of relationships. Genesis 2:18 conveys this assessment by our Creator: "It is not good for the man to be alone. I will make a helper suitable for him." Fellowship, personal relationships, and significant times of sharing are trademarks of a healthy disciple.

The Christian faith was designed to be lived in fellowship with other believers. The Acts 2:42 theme verse lists fellowship (*koinonia*) as one of the four basic foundation stones of the early church. It was one of the practices they devoted themselves to exercising regularly and systematically in their Christian calendar. The word *devoted* in this verse means to join, to adhere to, to connect, to experience together. In our vernacular we might say, they were "sticking together" in respect to the four activities listed in Acts 2:42, and one of those was fellowship.

How can I join together with others in my faith walk and have true fellowship and commonality? There are many ways this can be achieved. Some of them include joining a small group, enrolling in a Sunday School class, and participating in a group ministry such as choir or a church sports team. It is amazing how we bind ourselves together with others through a group activity. More intimate accountability groups, which typically involve three to five people take fellowship to a whole new level, for we engage with their strengths, weaknesses, joys, and sorrows. You may not be a social butterfly and may not feel comfortable joining group activities, but this is essential for Christian growth. Even the serving of the Lord's Supper or Holy Communion is a sharing of the remembrance of our Savior's death. The original word for our participation in this joint event is *koinonia*. Paul speaks of this commonality in 1 Corinthians 10:16, where he says that in this Communion we participate in the body and blood of Christ.

Think About It

The story is told about a man who disagreed with D.L. Moody on the importance of being together in worship and fellowship. The individual contended he did not need others but could live his life of faith quite well alone. A fire was burning in the room where the two men were holding this conversation. Moody proceeded to the fire and removed one log from the others. Both men watched as the log lost its bright orange hue and eventually burned out. The man quickly embraced the importance—indeed, the imperative—of being with others.

What This Means to You

You need to connect with other believers in order to maximize the growth potential you have in the kingdom of God. Also, your experiences and gifts can be invested in the lives of many other believers. Fellowship is a win-win proposition. Koinonia is a component of serving the King and strengthening your potential for influencing others for Jesus Christ.

Chapter 21
The Holy Spirit

Who is the Holy Spirit? What influence does He bring to bear upon my life?

What the Bible Has to Say

But you will receive power when the Holy Spirit comes on you; and you will be My witnesses in Jerusalem, and in all Judea and Samaria, and to the ends of the earth. (Acts 1:8)

The Holy Spirit, one of the three persons of the Trinity (Father, Son, and Holy Spirit), enables, empowers, and equips the believer to do the work of ministry. The Holy Spirit also convicts sinners and brings them to Jesus Christ the Savior.

The invisible nature of the Spirit was explained by Jesus with an analogy drawn from nature. The Spirit is like the wind; you cannot see it, but its reality is substantiated by what it does (see John 3:8–9). The symbols of the Holy Spirit as enumerated in Scripture are fire (Matthew 3:11), a dove (Matthew 3:16), wind (John 3:8), and water (John 7:37–39).

The Holy Spirit is a person. The Greek grammar for the word *spirit* is neuter (neither masculine nor feminine). However, in passages such as John 14:26, 15:26, and 16:13–14, the word for spirit (*pneuma*) has the masculine pronoun used with it, not the neuter. Personal activities such as speaking (Acts 8:29) and being grieved by sin (Ephesians 4:30) are attributed to the Holy Spirit.

What are the primary ministries of the Holy Spirit? The Spirit empowers men and women for service. First Samuel 16:13 reports, "So Samuel took the horn of oil and anointed him in the presence of his brothers, and from that day on the Spirit of the Lord came upon David in power." As the Spirit indwells the believer, the promise and prediction of Jesus in Acts 1:8 is fulfilled, "But you will receive power when the Holy Spirit comes on you; and you will be my witnesses in Jerusalem and in all Judea and Samaria, and to the ends of the earth."

This pouring out of the Spirit is sometimes labeled "the baptism of the Holy Spirit." The Spirit disperses gifts to believers as found in these words from Paul: "Now to each one the manifestation of the Spirit is given for the common good. To one there is given through the Spirit the message of wisdom, to another the message of knowledge by means of the same Spirit, to another faith by the same Spirit, to another gifts of healing by that one Spirit.... All these are the work of one and the same Spirit, and He gives them to each one, just as He determines" (1 Corinthians 12:7–9, 11).

The Spirit is involved with the purification and character of the believer. First Corinthians 6:11 shares these thoughts: "And that is what some of you were. But you were washed, you were sanctified, you were justified in the name of the Lord Jesus Christ and by the Spirit of our God."

Holy and righteous living is fostered by the fruit of the Spirit: "But the fruit of the Spirit is love, joy, peace, patience, kindness, goodness, faithfulness, gentleness and self-control. Against such things there is no law" (Galatians 5:22–23).

The Holy Spirit engages in a revealing ministry. The writers of God's Word were escorted by the Spirit: "For prophecy never had its origin in the will of man, but men spoke from God as they were carried along by the Holy Spirit" (2 Peter 1:21).

The assurance of our salvation is offered by the third person of the Trinity: "The Spirit Himself testifies with our spirit that we are God's children" (Romans 8:16).

The Spirit of God teaches God's people: "But the Counselor, the Holy Spirit, whom the Father will send in my name, will teach you all things and will remind you of everything I have said to you" (John 14:26).

And the Holy Spirit also convicts God's people: "When He comes, He will convict the world of guilt in regard to sin and righteousness and judgment" (John 16:8).

Finally, the Holy Spirit is a cohesive agent to unify the church. Paul encourages the Ephesians, "Make every effort to keep the unity of the Spirit through the bond of peace" (Ephesians 4:3). Also, in 2 Corinthians 13:14, he ends with this benediction: "May the grace of the Lord Jesus Christ, and the love of God, and the fellowship of the Holy Spirit be with you all."

The Holy Spirit is coequal and coeternal with the Father and the Son and fulfills a number of roles to bring glory to the Godhead and to build the church.

Think About It

The concept of the Trinity (or "God in three persons")—Father, Son, and Holy Spirit—is a mystery. How can God be one and three at the same time? The analogy of a container of water is helpful. If the temperatures in the container range from freezing at one end to boiling at the other, the body of water in a single moment of time can be solid, liquid, and gas. One substance, in one second of time, with different temperatures, can exist in three expressions.

What This Means to You

The Holy Spirit is the Christian's invisible partner. He is like the wind that you cannot see, yet you are able to see the results. The Holy Spirit lives inside the believer working to transform each disciple into the image of Jesus Christ.

Chapter 22
Spiritual Gifts

How do I discover my spiritual gifts?

What the Bible Has to Say

Each one should use whatever gift he has received to serve others, faithfully administering God's grace in its various forms. (1 Peter 4:10)

C. Peter Wagner defines a spiritual gift as "a special attribute given by the Holy Spirit to every member of the Body of Christ, according to God's grace, for use within the context of the Body." This gifting is not for unbelievers but is an important part of the believer's ministry. Spiritual gifts are not natural talents, such as the ability to hit a baseball or run fast. The Lord can use our natural talents for His glory, but they are different from spiritual gifts. Spiritual gifts are also not the same as the fruit of the Spirit listed in Galatians 5:22–23.

Where can you find a list of the spiritual gifts? Check these four key chapters of the New Testament: Romans 12, 1 Corinthians 12, Ephesians 4, and 1 Peter 4. These gifts range from mercy to missionary, from pastor to prophet, and they provide a wide assortment for the believer to study and consider.

There are several steps you can take to discover your spiritual gift(s). Study the gift chapters, and pray to the Lord for discernment regarding what gifts you have been given. You can also take a spiritual gift survey, which will point you toward the particular gifts the Holy Spirit has deposited in your life. A pastor or church leader should be able to provide this tool.

Once you believe you've identified your gifts, try them out. For example, if teaching seems to fit you, volunteer to teach a class. If mercy is your gift, volunteer to help someone in need. If you've correctly identified you gifts, then your efforts will be a blessing to you and others. Also, you may want to seek out mature believers for their assessment of your potential gifts. Identifying and using your gifts will be a gratifying pursuit and can result in your life multiplying its effectiveness in many others within God's family.

Think About It

Charles Swindoll tells the story of a group of animals that started a school to improve their overall success in life. The curriculum included such skills as swimming, running, climbing, and flying. Though it sounded like a great idea, it was doomed to failure. The squirrel got an *A* in climbing, but his overall grade dropped to a *C* because his instructors spent hours trying to teach him how to swim and fly. The eagle was placed in a remedial class in climbing, even though flying was his strong suit. What a waste of time. Believers need to discover their gifts and deploy them in the ministry areas where they will be most productive.

What This Means to You

It is important that you discover your spiritual gifts so that you can grow as a believer, contribute to the health of the church, and bring glory to God for the gifts He has given to us through the Holy Spirit.

Chapter 23
The Lordship of Jesus Christ

What does it mean that Jesus is Lord of my life?

What the Bible Has to Say

Therefore let all Israel be assured of this: God has made this Jesus whom you crucified, both Lord and Christ. (Acts 2:36)

The Bible is clear that Jesus not only fulfills the role of Savior but also of Lord. This word may not receive a warm welcome in a culture populated by people who want to control their own destiny and be self-directed, self-sufficient, and self-motivated.

Lordship means one follows the call and commands of another. Lordship means we are the passengers and Jesus is the driver. Lordship means Jesus reigns and we are His servants. There are many who are willing to call Jesus their *Savior*, because doing so proclaims He has done something for us, but Lordship focuses on how we will serve Him.

Paul's letter to the Romans covers the theme of salvation—how an individual can be saved. Notice how many times the word *Lord* appears in this strategic passage of Scripture. Paul wrote, "If you confess with your mouth 'Jesus is Lord' and believe in your heart that God raised Him from the dead, you will be saved. For it is with your heart that you believe and are justified, and it is with your mouth that you confess and are saved. As the Scripture says, 'Anyone who trusts in Him will never be put to shame.' For there is no difference between Jew and Gentile—the same Lord is Lord of all and richly blesses all who call on His name, for, 'Everyone who calls on the name of the Lord will be saved'" (Romans 10:9–13).

In this salvation passage, the word *Lord* is mentioned four times. Charles Spurgeon, the great English author and preacher, claimed that "If Christ is not all to you He is nothing to you. He will never go into partnership as a part Savior of men. If He be something He must be everything, and if He be not everything He is nothing to you." Spurgeon emphatically believed that Jesus Christ cannot be your Savior without being your Lord. The two roles, Savior and Lord, are part of one package.

Another vital passage on the Lordship of Jesus and His absolute sovereignty over our lives is found in Paul's letter to the church at Corinth: "Now about the gifts of the Spirit, brothers and sisters, I do not want you to be uninformed. You know that when you were pagans, somehow or other you were influenced and led astray to mute idols. Therefore I want you to know that no one who is speaking by the Spirit of God says, 'Jesus be cursed,' and no one can say, 'Jesus is Lord,' except by the Holy Spirit" (1 Corinthians 12:1–3).

The Holy Spirit moves us to give Jesus His due as Lord. Those who are born into God's kingdom do not curse Jesus; rather they affirm the Lordship of Jesus. The original word here is used in the Septuagint, the Greek translation of the Old Testament, to translate the Hebrew name, *Yahweh, the Lord,* the name God told Moses to proclaim to the Israelites; the name of God. Yahweh means, "I Am." The expanded meaning of I Am is that God is declaring, "I am everything you need, I am Lord of all!"

Jesus expects full compliance and full commitment as evidenced by His call, "Then he said to them all: 'If anyone would come after me, he must deny himself and take up his cross daily and follow me. For whoever wants to save his life will lose it, but whoever loses his life for me will save it'" (Luke 9:23-24). Because He is Lord, Jesus can demand this type of investment. He owns all the deeds of our existence, even our very lives.

Think About It

The story is told of the cathedral in Freiburg, Germany, which contained a famous organ. One day a man entered and asked to play it. The custodian resisted the request, but he eventually granted permission. The guest sat down and began to play music which moved the sexton to take a seat and eventually the man began to weep over the beautiful sounds that emerged from the instrument he was entrusted to care for and guard. When the stranger stood up and began to leave, the custodian inquired, "Who are you?"

The visitor replied, "I am Mendelssohn."

The old man threw up his hands and cried, "And to think I almost refused to let you play my organ."

When Jesus Christ enters our lives, He turns disharmony to harmony and noise to music. He tunes us, removing the sins which cause discordant and displeasing sounds. However, He does not want to merely tune our instrument; He wants to play it.

What This Means to You

Your life "roots" must draw water from Christ's life and the Holy Spirit. As you imitate Jesus and obey His commands, as you pursue his model and motivation, as you submit and surrender to Him, you will become more like Him and demonstrate that He is your Lord.

Chapter 24
The Will of God

*How do I discover God's will and what are the consequences
if I can't discern it or if I disobey it?*

What the Bible Has to Say

*For I have come down from heaven not to do My will but to do the will
of Him who sent Me.* (John 6:38)

The will of God is a critical issue in the believer's walk with Jesus. Our
theme verse, John 6:38, asserts that Christ's goal on earth was to follow
and fulfill God's will. Can we do any less if we are to "walk as Jesus
walked" (1 John 2:6)?

When Jesus wrestled in the garden of Gethsemane with the bitter
cup of death, He came to this resolution: "My Father, if it is possible,
may this cup be taken from Me. Yet not as I will, but as You will"
(Matthew 26:39).

Jesus took God's will seriously. And in the Sermon on the Mount, He
articulated its seriousness for each of us: "Not everyone who says to
me, 'Lord, Lord,' will enter the kingdom of heaven, but only he who
does the will of my Father who is in heaven'" (Matthew 7:21). Doing
the will of God is a determining factor in whether an individual enters

heaven or is kept out of it. So, how do I discern what God's will is for my life?

Since the Bible does not tell the disciple of Jesus what to do in every situation, at every intersection, we might describe it more like a compass that gives us direction rather than a road map that tells us every turn we are to take on our trip.

Here are seven guideposts that point us toward God's will for our individual lives. These seven indicators enable us to have a clearer picture of what the Lord desires us to do:

1. *Read and Study the Bible*: God has written the Bible so that we may be exposed to His holy mind and heart. He has produced a manual for living. The Bible is the most reliable instrument on the dashboard of our lives, and it functions like "a lamp to my feet and a light to my path" (Psalm 119:105).

2. *Consider the Circumstances*: Open doors and closed doors are often used by the Lord to show us His way and mark out His path. An example of this is found in Paul's decision to tarry in a certain place rather than move on to another city. In 1 Corinthians 16:8-9 he wrote, "But I will stay on at Ephesus until Pentecost, because a great door for effective work has opened to me."

3. *Listen to the Inner Witness of the Holy Spirit*: The Holy Spirit, who lives within each of us, is like a built-in travel guide. The Spirit leads us by instilling peace or turmoil in our heart as we seek to make decisions. This is the still small voice, the gentle whisper, that guided Elijah the prophet. The Apostle

Paul highlights this navigational role of the Spirit in Romans 8:14: "Because those who are led by the Spirit of God are sons of God."

4. *Seek Wise Counsel*: Seasoned believers can assist other believers in discerning God's will. Listening to advice is a godly attribute, as proposed in Proverbs 12:15: "The way of a fool seems right to him, but a wise man listens to advice." Multiple counselors are recommended, as endorsed by Proverbs 24:6: "For waging war you need guidance, and for victory many advisors."

5. *Reflect on Personal Desires*: Don't discount the leanings of your heart in a certain direction. "Delight yourself in the Lord and He will give you the desires of your heart" is the promise of Psalm 37:4. Notice this granting of our desires is tied to delighting in the Lord, and when we engage in that activity, this is what happens: His desires become our desires—therefore, they are always granted.

6. *Use Common Sense*: This is a valuable asset for one who is trying to ascertain God's will. The Lord wants us to use the minds He equipped us with to think through decisions. When the prodigal son squandered all his inheritance, he ended up in a pigpen eating slop. Luke 15:17 reports that "he came to his senses," reasoning it was better to go back to his father and be a well-taken-care-of servant than a son relegated to the life of a pig in a foreign country. That makes common sense.

7. *Don't Rule Out Special Guidance*: This is when an angel taps you on the shoulder, or an audible voice from heaven speaks

to you like Paul was spoken to in Acts 9. Be careful, for this type of guidance is rare; however, God can employ whatever means He desires to capture our attention and point us to the proper path.

One more thought: God's will is not always dark and distasteful. Often it places us in pleasant places (Psalm 16:6). David asserted in Psalm 40:8, "I desire to do your will, O my God."

Think About It

When we come to a crossroads in our lives and need to make a decision, we must be careful we don't utilize bizarre means to arrive at our choice of paths. One man could not decide what color of car he would buy. He kept bumping into the color yellow, so he determined the Lord wanted him to buy a yellow car. He ended up with a lemon.

What This Means to You

Discerning God's will for your life is sometimes plainly prescribed in His Word, but often it requires persistent prayer and wrestling with several alternatives. However, the outcome is worth the effort. Perhaps the seven guideposts will serve you well in discovering God's will for your life and work! One book that has been beneficial to me in trying to decode the will of God is Garry Friesen's book, *Decision Making and the Will of God*.

Chapter 25
Prayer

What is the meaning of prayer?
How do I practice this spiritual discipline?

What the Bible Has to Say

And pray in the Spirit on all occasions with all kinds of prayer and requests. With this in mind, be alert and always keep on praying for all the saints. (Ephesians 6:18)

Prayer can be simply defined as "conversation with God." This working definition extends from Gregory of Nyssa, an early church father, to Bill Bright, the founder of Campus Crusade. Since it is a conversation, prayer involves both talking and listening. This dialogue with the divine is a distinct privilege for the believer. Think about this: Christians have the distinct honor of communicating with Someone who transcends all others, who can be reached at any place, any time, and who understands every piece of information that is given to Him.

Prayer is indispensable in the life of the believer. It is as critical as fuel to an engine, ammunition to a weapon, or air to the lungs. John Bunyan, the author of *Pilgrim's Progress*, wrote: "You can do more than pray, after you have prayed, but you cannot do more than pray until you have prayed." Paul, in the theme verse cited above, instructed those followers of Jesus to pray on all occasions and with all kinds of prayers. In Luke 18:1, our Lord "told His disciples a parable to show them that they should always pray and not give up."

The richest encyclopedia on the practice of prayer is found in the life and ministry of our Lord Jesus Christ. Fifteen of His prayers are recorded in the four Gospels. He prays at the beginning of His ministry and during His crucifixion. He prays early in the morning and late at night. He prays with joyful thanksgiving before a miracle and with painful agony in the garden of Gethsemane. If Jesus found prayer so effective and so necessary, can His followers diminish its frequency and prominence in Christian living? The poet Tennyson made this stunning assessment: "More things are wrought by prayer than this world dreams of."

And don't be timid to ask God in prayer. Charles Spurgeon, the great preacher and writer from England, declared that "asking is the rule of the Kingdom." The idea was not original with him; Jesus commanded in Matthew 7:7–8, "Ask and it will be given to you; seek and you will find; knock and the door will be opened to you. For everyone who asks receives; he who seeks finds; and to him who knocks, the door will be opened."

Sometimes you may find it hard to get started in prayer. Here are two useful acrostic models for prayer, ACTS and PRAY:

      A (adoration)

      C (confession)

      T (thanksgiving for specific items)

      S (supplications, or requests for specific needs)

and

> **P** (praise)
>
> **R** (repent)
>
> **A** (asking for others)
>
> **Y** (ask for yourself)

One final point should be made: when we pray, we must believe that God can and will answer. James 1:6–7 challenges us with these words: "But when he asks, he must believe and not doubt, because he who doubts is like a wave of the sea, blown and tossed by the wind. That man should not think he will receive anything from the Lord." Faith is imperative when we pray. This principle is echoed in Hebrew 11:6: "And without faith it is impossible to please God, because anyone who comes to Him must believe that He exists and that He rewards those who earnestly seek Him."

Prayer + Faith = a winning equation.

Think About It

The comparison between prayer and an electric wiring system is appropriate. Electric current is available and must be turned on. A switch is the trigger, and if moved even slightly, current surges through the whole house. Not much power is required to flip a switch, but a tremendous wattage of power is released through electric currents. The dynamics of God are available when we pray. If you think of prayer as a small, insignificant exercise, just remember the switch.

What This Means to You

Andrew Murray wrote, "Prayer is the one hand with which we grasp the invisible."

A.B. Simpson defined prayer in this pictorial way: "The hand of the child touches the arm of the Father and moves the wheels of the universe."

Many believers have made reference to the familiar axiom, "Prayer changes things," and that is true. However, if you practice prayer on a daily basis, you will also discover prayer changes people, for it will certainly change you.

Chapter 26
The Lord's Prayer

What is the significance of the Lord's Prayer?

What the Bible Has to Say

One day Jesus was praying in a certain place. When He finished, one of His disciples said to Him, "Lord, teach us to pray just as John taught his disciples." (Luke 11:1)

The Lord's model prayer was given in response to a request made by His disciples following their observation of Him praying. The prayer is also recorded in Matthew, which is its fullest form, and this passage will be used as the foundation for teaching on this most popular prayer in the entire Bible. It is a paradigm to follow as believers seek to praise and petition God in their life of prayer:

> *Our Father in heaven,*
> *hallowed be your name,*
> *your kingdom come,*
> *your will be done*
> *on earth as it is in heaven.*

> *Give us today our daily bread.*
> *Forgive us our debts,*
> *as we also have forgiven our debtors.*
> *And lead us not into temptation,*
> *but deliver us from the evil one.* (Matthew 6:9-13)

Jesus made a revolutionary change in the greeting He prescribed for the model prayer. He begins with the words, "Our Father." This was a new twist, for the Jewish people did not address God intimately in a family sense. According to Jesus, God is now to be addressed as a child addresses his father. Both Jesus and Paul used the word *Abba* to speak to God in prayer, and this is even more astonishing, for the most precise translation of Abba is *Daddy*. We are to pray to God with the simple trust, innocence, and confidence of a child who comes to his father, the source of his provision and protection. In eight of the nine recorded prayers of Jesus Christ, He greets God as Father.

Jesus completes His greeting with "in heaven." Yes, God is the intimate Father, but He is also transcendent. "In heaven," speaks of the otherness of God, His distinct role above and beyond all His creation and creatures.

The model prayer follows the greeting with emphasis on three praise priorities of God the Father, namely, His glorious name, His kingdom that reigns, and His will.

According to Jesus's model, praise precedes petition.

"Hallowed be your name," highlights the principle of God's glory. The root word for hallowed, the Greek word, *hagiazo*, means to set apart.

The word is used for sanctify in the New Testament. In our prayers, we are to demonstrate a reverence of God's name and character. God is not just a "buddy."

"Your kingdom come," points to His reign over our hearts and ultimately over all earth and heaven. The kingdom is a dynamic concept, one which encompasses the past, present, and future. The kingdom is now, but not yet. The kingdom is here in us, but we await its final consummation. The kingdom is present in its early stages, but God's final establishment of His kingdom is not yet complete.

"Your will be done" is a centerpiece of God's concerns. The Father's will is to supersede our will. Our wills must be swallowed up by God's will. God's will is sometimes painful, sometimes pleasant, but always perfect. Jesus wrestled with this principle in the garden of Gethsemane just before His crucifixion on the cross. He asked three times to not drink the "cup of suffering," but finally, surrendering in prayer, He stated, "Not my will, but yours be done" (Luke 22:42). Such is the response of the obedient disciple.

The model prayer follows God's concerns with man's personal concerns and needs. "Give us today our daily bread," is the first request of human need. There is nothing spiritually wrong with making petition for our daily food and provision. To refuse to pray for these needs leads to spiritual pride and independence. Daily bread is a function of the Father on behalf of His children.

"Forgive us our debts [sins]," is a crucial component of our prayer menu. Jesus places at the center of man's concerns the purification of his heart. It is God's highest pleasure to heal us of our spiritual cancer. One word of caution: the prayer includes the qualifier, "as we have also forgiven our debtors." Augustine, the great church father, labeled this "the terrible petition." God expects us to forgive others in the manner He has forgiven us.

It was General Oglethorpe who said to John Wesley, "I will never forgive."

"Then I hope, sir," Wesley replied, "you never sin."

Those who are forgiven are to be forgiving people.

"Lead us not into temptation, but deliver us from evil," is the final concern for man in this three-fold petition. Jesus, in His high-priestly prayer, highlighted this concern again: "My prayer is not that you take them out of the world but that you protect them from the evil one" (John 17:15). Even Jesus was tempted by the devil. But we as believers are encouraged by Paul's words in 1 Corinthians 10:13: "No temptation has seized you except what is common to man. And God is faithful; He will not let you be tempted beyond what you cannot bear. But when you are tempted, He will also provide a way out so that you can stand up under it." When temptation comes through the front door of your life, look for the window of escape that God will provide.

Many late manuscripts of the Lord's Prayer end with a doxology, a word of praise to God: "For yours is the kingdom and the power and the glory forever. Amen." It accentuates the reign of God and His ability to sustain the regency and the glory due Him because of His kingship in history and beyond.

Think About It

Dennis Kinlaw, former President of Asbury College, remarked following the Asbury Revival of 1970, which started and spread among the students of the college and extended throughout America, "Give me one divine moment when God acts and I say that moment is superior to all the human efforts of man throughout the centuries." Prayer is the key to open the door to many of these moments.

What This Means to You

The Lord's Prayer or Model Prayer provides a blueprint for Christians in every generation. Many have discounted prayer to their regret, but those who participate in prayer have access to the power and provision of God.

Chapter 27
Accountability

Is it important for me to have an accountability partner?

What the Bible Has to Say

As iron sharpens iron, so one man sharpens another. (Proverbs 27:17)

The New Testament speaks of the group dynamic in such verses as Hebrews 10:24, which states: "And let us consider how we may spur one another on toward love and good deeds." There are over thirty "one another" passages in the New Testament. It is crucial that men and women build systems of accountability into the fiber and fabric of their lives. The maxim, "two are better than one," comes directly from the Scriptures (Ecclesiastes 4:9).

Accountability relationships are featured throughout Scripture with such pairs as Abraham and Lot, Elijah and Elisha, and Paul and Timothy. These pairs in the Holy Book spared men and nations from catastrophic disaster.

I have an accountability partner I meet with on a regular basis. I have chosen someone who is not in the church that I pastor. We gather for a breakfast meal, prayer, and a time of asking each other questions and sharing on various topics that are pertinent to our lives. My accountability partner has requested I ask two specific questions each time we meet.

Question One: "What have you looked at since the last time we met?"

Question Two: "What is happening in your devotional life?"

These two questions bring to the surface many issues that can prevent my brother from engaging in activities that are displeasing to God and destructive to him and his family. Because we have made an agreement, he is fully aware these questions are coming to him at every accountability meeting. That gives him an incentive to live with his heart and mind "set on things above" (Col. 3:1–2). My friend asks me questions pertaining to my family, my ministry, and my relationship with the Lord. He has kept me from frustration, from making a serious ministry error, and has kept me far more balanced than I would ever be on my own. There is a part of us that regrets at times the answers we must give in response to the questions, but there are no regrets regarding the value of such an experience for cultivating a more fully devoted disciple of Jesus Christ.

There are many accountability models that lay out a list of questions two or more individuals could ask each other in a small group setting. *Emerge Ministries,* a successful counseling institute in Akron, Ohio, provides eight sample questions that could be used in a regular accountability relationship. These questions are as follows:

1. Have you been with anyone, anywhere, that would appear as compromising?

2. Have you entertained any inappropriate fantasies in your thought life?

3. Have you viewed or read any sexually explicit material?

4. Have any of your financial dealings lacked integrity?

5. Have you spent adequate time in Bible study and prayer?

6. Have you given priority time to your family?

7. Have you been faithful to your commission of Christian service?

8. Have you just lied to me?

Think About It

In *Blue Like Jazz*, Donald Miller wrote, "Sometimes I think, you know, if there were not cops, I would be fine, and I probably would. I was taught right from wrong when I was a kid. But the truth is, I drive completely different when there is a cop behind me than when there isn't" (p. 18).

What This Means to You

A Dallas Theological Seminary study discovered that 250 pastors who fell into sin had one striking constant: *They had no accountability partner or system.* If two are better than one, then it is incumbent on us to find someone we can share with in an accountability relationship.

Don't place yourself in a precarious position. Howard Hendricks, a Dallas Theological Seminary professor and best-selling author, once remarked, "A man who is not in a group with another man is an accident waiting to happen."

Chapter 28
Money

What are the Lord's expectations regarding a believer's use of money?

What the Bible Has to Say

No one can serve two masters. Either he will hate the one and love the other, or he will be devoted to the one and despise the other. You cannot serve both God and Money. (Matthew 6:24)

The theme verse is a fascinating one because it contends money can be the master of our lives, and our devotion to it can compete for the preeminence God is to hold in our hearts. In other words, money can become a god. Our possessions, including money, jewelry, land, houses, and other material things, fall under the concept we call *stewardship*. We must embrace the truth that everything we own is the Lord's. Psalm 24:1 states, "The earth is the Lord's and everything in it, the world, and all who live in it." This means God owns all the deeds in our lives and we are not owners, but managers or stewards.

It may surprise you that stewardship appears over two thousand times in the Bible, more than heaven or hell, more than faith or prayer.

Therefore, we may conclude it is extremely important to exercise discipline in this critical area.

One particular tool the Lord has provided to help us manage money (rather than letting money manage us) is the concept of *tithing*. The Hebrew and Greek words for this mean a tenth. The tithe, this 10 percent benchmark, honors the Lord by giving Him the firstfruits of earnings. This concept is woven throughout the Bible. The tithe was begun by Abraham even before the law (Genesis 14:20), confirmed by Jacob (Genesis 28:22), commanded in the law (Deuteronomy 14:22), commended with a promise (Proverbs 3:9), promoted as a corporate (church) and individual living principle in the final book of the Old Testament (Malachi 3:10), reaffirmed by Jesus Christ in the New Testament (Matthew 23:23) and is to be undertaken, as all kingdom giving, with a cheerful spirit, as emphasized by Paul (2 Corinthians 9:7).

The passage in Malachi is especially instructive. God accuses His people of robbing Him. "But you ask, 'How do we rob You?' In tithes and offerings. You are under a curse—the whole nation of you—because you are robbing Me. Bring the whole tithe into the storehouse, that there may be food in my house. Test Me in this," says the Lord Almighty, "and see if I will not throw open the floodgates of heaven and pour out so much blessing that you will not have room enough for it" (Malachi 3:8–10).

These verses compose an indictment ("you are robbing Me"), a commandment ("Bring the tithe"), and a promise ("so much blessing that you will not have room to receive it"). The tithe, the first 10 percent, is sacred. It is to be brought to the storehouse, meaning where you are spiritually fed. Then, the Lord provides an overwhelming blessing that goes beyond any receptacle we could provide to receive His favor. When we tithe we form a partnership with the Lord, and we are saying, "I can live on 90 percent with the Lord a lot better than 100 percent without Him." This type of stewardship is a faith venture that sets us apart from a secular culture and places us in obedience to God's plan for our money and other possessions.

Think About It

Riches are like birds in a man's backyard. Just because they are sitting there does not mean they can't fly away.

What This Means to You

Money can be a terrific tool to glorify God, take care of your family, and meet the needs of those who are hurting. It can also be a terrible tyrant in your life. The first pathway is one of great blessing and gratification; the second pathway is one of great cursing and destruction. Choose wisely.

Chapter 29
Anger

Is anger always a negative part of my portfolio?
Can anger be used for God's glory?

What the Bible Has to Say

In your anger do not sin. Do not let the sun go down while you are still angry.... Get rid of all bitterness, rage and anger, brawling and slander, along with every form of malice. (Ephesians 4:26, 31)

Anger is a part of the human personality. Before we come to faith in Christ, anger will appear in destructive expressions. Even after we surrender our sins to Jesus Christ our Savior, we still will manifest it. Anger can be a righteous act when it is triggered by our sensitivity to sin and our efforts to avoid it, eliminate it, or perhaps enable another to forsake evil and to pursue godliness.

The word translated "anger" in Ephesians 4:26 is not describing the kind of emotion that boils up and quickly subsides (*thumos*). This may occur if someone bumps into our car in a parking lot. Although our emotions spike, we quickly realize the person driving the other car was not aiming at our vehicle—it was an accident.

Or suppose one of our children trips in the living room and destroys a family heirloom. We may have invested much sentiment into the item, but hopefully we will remember all the items we broke when we were children, and the angry flare-up will die down to a small disappointment.

Now, a different word for anger is used in Ephesians 4:26—*orge*. Kenneth Wuest, a noted New Testament Greek scholar of the mid-twentieth century, defines *orge* as "an abiding and settled habit of the mind that is aroused under certain conditions." The anger Paul is speaking of is a righteous anger that is constantly angry with sin. Jesus exhibited righteous anger when He was about to heal the shriveled hand of a man in the synagogue and the Pharisees, rather than hoping for a miracle, were looking for a reason to accuse Jesus of doing wrong on the Sabbath day. The Scriptures report, "He looked around at them in anger (*orge*) and, deeply distressed at their stubborn hearts, said to the man, 'Stretch out your hand.' He stretched it out, and his hand was completely restored" (Mark 3:5). God exhibits righteous anger. In fact, Psalm 7:11 links His righteousness with His anger, and this anger is vented "every day."

However, if anger does not take a time out, if it continues beyond sunset, it could cross the line into a dark anger that never forgives, never lets go of its passion. Anger counseling has escalated dramatically in our time and anger's power to destroy has become more widespread. Proverbs 14:17 warns that, "A quick-tempered man does foolish things." Again in Proverbs, designated as the wisdom book, we encounter this solemn truth: "A hot-tempered man must pay the penalty; if you rescue him, you will have to do it again" (19:19).

Believers can struggle with this emotion, and though it should be exercised repeatedly against sin, it must not be incessantly repeated in its unacceptable form. Paul Tripp, in the video series *How to be Good and Angry,* asserts, "If you ever want to understand your anger, you have to look this way (inward), because your anger is connected not just to events outside of you; your anger is connected to something going on inside of you. You will never gain ground with your anger unless you get this."

Think About It

Here is a worthy thought to consider: Godly people get angry but they manage it—it does not manage them. If they don't, the devil sees an opportunity (Ephesians 4:27). Don't let him get a foot into the door of your heart.

What This Means to You

Anger can be a commendable arrow in the arsenal of your Christian quiver. Jesus used it effectively against the Pharisees. It can also be a destructive bullet in the legacy you are attempting to leave behind. In Numbers 20:8-13, Moses is angered at the Hebrews for their lack of faith. God had instructed him to speak to a rock so that water would satisfy the complaints of a thirsty people. However, in his rage, Moses struck the rock twice, thereby, disobeying God. He was forbidden from entering the Promised Land with his people during his lifetime because of this outburst of anger.

Chapter 30
Social Media

Can social media be a hindrance to my Christian growth?

What the Bible Has to Say

Everything is permissible—but not everything is beneficial. Everything is permissible—but not everything is constructive. (1 Corinthians 10:23)

Twitter and Facebook are instruments of *social media*. They allow people to connect with others at work, home, school, or any other venue. In the theme verse, Paul makes a significant point that certain aspects of our lives are permissible to experience or use, but that does not make them always an asset. Social media sites are morally neutral—they have no inherent value, neither good nor evil. For instance, a knife is neutral. In the hand of a surgeon, a knife can help save a life, but in the hand of a murderer, it can be employed to take a life.

Social media can be used to communicate prayer requests or answers to prayer, for example. However, if overused and especially if used to communicate trivia such as, "I'm brushing my teeth," social media sites can consume time we could spend in productive living. This technology can steal valuable time and opportunities to enhance our lives and the lives of many others.

Paul wrote to the church in Ephesus, "Be very careful, then, how you live—not as unwise but as wise, making the most of every opportunity, because the days are evil" (Ephesians 5:15–16). We are investors who have been given a precious commodity—time—and we must be discerning in how we invest it for dividends. We must monitor our expenditures of time, or our lives may become unproductive.

The quality of relationships may be diminished by the use of social media. There are significant relationships, and there are casual relationships. If we retreat into the world of social media, we may find our days eaten up with an overwhelming barrage of trivial messages rather than meeting people face-to-face and having discussions that are important and strategic. Social media cannot duplicate the dialogue that transpires when we meet face-to-face. This personal exchange is so crucial to our development as social beings who not only read what others say, but hear, see, and touch others in a live and ongoing relationship.

Matthew 18:15–18 details how to approach a person who has sinned against us—in other words, they have spoken or done something that brought an offense to our relationship. The prescription of the Lord starts with the offended party meeting the offending party in person.

A respected pastor taught me that if you want to say something positive to a person, write it down and send them a message. This demonstrates you thought it important enough to craft a compliment or thank you that takes more effort than merely saying thank you.

However, if your message is to correct an individual or to point out something that was hurtful or inappropriate, you should meet with them in person. I have discovered this advice to be beneficial in my own ministry with others.

Think About It

How many of the five senses are involved in social media? How many senses are involved in a person-to-person conversation?

There are times when social media is helpful, but in a relational sense, these modern technologies often fall short in developing depth with others, by consuming too much of our time with trivial pursuits.

What This Means to You

Social media sites are a component of our modern age. However, make sure you manage them, or they will manage you. They may be permissible, but they may not increase your productivity for the Lord, or for your family, friends, and fellow employees.

Chapter 31
Friends

*How influential is my circle of friends in regard to
being more or less like Jesus Christ?*

What the Bible Has to Say

Do not be misled: "Bad company spoils good character."
(1 Corinthians 15:33)

The apostle Paul is instructing the Corinthians on the dangers of traveling in a pagan circle of friends. His quotation is from a Greek comedy written by Menander, and it is here applied to flash a warning light that our group of associates can contaminate our character and bring us down. The choice of our herd or huddle will have a profound impact on the quality of our faith life. When I instructed our two sons about who they were going to date or even more significantly who they were going to marry, I advised them to ask the question, "Will this young lady be an asset or liability to me following Jesus Christ?" No one can escape the impact friends will have on our health and holiness. It really does matter who we travel with most often.

Life is like a photograph: it is as important what or who you leave out of the picture as what and who you allow in it. Psalm 1 speaks directly to the negative influence friends can have upon your life. This Psalm begins by promising a blessing to those who avoid people who are ungodly. "Blessed is the man who does not walk in the counsel of the wicked or stand in the way of sinners or sit in the seat of the scornful" (Psalm 1:1).

This verse features a progression of involvement with the ungodly that comprises a series of red flags. First, a man walks with the ungodly, then he stands with the ungodly, and finally he sits down with them. The relationship progresses from casual to conversational, and then to confined, where the victim is now no longer moving but is in an entrenched position.

Our circle of friends sooner or later becomes a circle of counselors. Whether this is a good or bad factor is directly related to the kind of friends we have in our sphere of influence. "As iron sharpens iron, so one man sharpens another" (Proverbs 27:17), but dull iron makes for dull iron. Proverbs 24:6 offers this advice for battle: "For waging war you need guidance, and for victory many advisers." Life is not a game; it is truly a battle. Our ears must be tuned to those who are competent in their understanding of the Bible and who are mature in living out its precepts.

You must choose wisely the herd you run with, for it will change you for better or worse. You may need to disassociate yourself from some acquaintances and move yourself into fellowship with those you trust as mature believers, who can positively affect you and advise you. This is difficult but necessary. The Bible heroes made both redemptive and destructive decisions regarding their friends. Samson's choice to associate with the woman Delilah led to his tragic downfall. Though he was the strongest man on the planet physically, Delilah's female charm and evil intention to profit from sharing Samson's secret for strength with his enemies led to the end of his role as a Hebrew judge—indeed, it shortened his life. We must choose wisely the huddle of our lives.

Think About It

Someone has wisely observed, "In five years you will be a product of the books you read and the friends you associate with." Check your library and assess your schedule, and you will have a clear understanding of what you will be in sixty months.

What This Means to You

You cannot choose your relatives, but you can choose your friends. Please listen carefully: you will be shaped and molded by those you spend the most time with and those you share the most life events with. Choose wisely.

Chapter 32
Fitness

What is the Bible's position on physical fitness? How do the Scriptures compare the value of physical fitness with spiritual fitness?

What the Bible Has to Say

For physical training is of some value, but godliness has value for all things, holding promise for both the present life and the life to come (1 Timothy 4:8).

The Christian faith speaks to both physical fitness and spiritual fitness. As you would expect, the spiritual side of the equation is weighted heavier than the physical side. First Timothy 4:8 assigns to the physical side "some value" but applauds the spiritual with "value for all things" and extends its worth to both this present life and eternal life.

What does God's Word say about caring for our bodies? Paul elevated the place of the body by describing it as the "temple" or "house" of the Holy Spirit. He wrote in 1 Corinthians 6:19–20, "Do you not know that your bodies are temples of the Holy Spirit, who is in you, whom you have received from God? You are not your own; you were bought at a price. Therefore honor God with your bodies."

In a related text, 1 Corinthians 3:17, Paul spoke of our bodies as holy, "If anyone destroys God's temple, God will destroy that person; for God's temple is sacred, and you together are that temple." Paul was dealing with a heresy called Gnosticism. This belief system stated that the body was corrupt and many Gnostics believed you could indulge in any activity with the body because it was beyond redemption or holiness since all matter was evil. The disciple of Jesus takes a much different perspective and looks at the care of the body as a stewardship issue since it is the temple.

Christians are called to discipline the body so that they are not vulnerable to certain sins. Overeating, over-drinking, and sexual infidelity are some of the temptations that could adversely affect a Christian who does not take care of his "temple."

In 1 Corinthians 9:27, Paul provides a warning: "No, I strike a blow to my body and make it my slave so that after I have preached to others, I myself will not be disqualified for the prize." He understood the liabilities of mistreating or neglecting the body because it could leave the door open for spiritual failure.

In Romans 12:1 Paul framed our care of our bodies in these terms: "Therefore, I urge you, brothers and sisters, in view of God's mercy, to offer your bodies as a living sacrifice, holy and pleasing to God—this is your true and proper worship." Caring for our bodies is an act of worship to God.

We can conclude that exercise has not only physical but also spiritual implications. Exercise, strength, and good health provide more energy, more years of service, and more opportunity to witness for Jesus. Physical strength is related to productivity in the spiritual realm. Proverbs 31:17, the passage describing "the excellent woman," commends her for her muscles, "She sets about her work vigorously; her arms are strong for her tasks."

Don't discount that walking and weights may add to your spiritual stamina and your ability to achieve certain tasks God has assigned you. What kind of regimen or routine do you have to take care of your temple? Being a couch potato is not funny because it opens the door for diminished effectiveness, a shortened life of service, and the opportunity for temptation to triumph.

Granted, spiritual fitness is more valuable and must be a higher and stronger focus of the believer's life. As the philosopher Pierre Teilhard de Chardin noted, "We are not human beings having a spiritual experience, we are spiritual beings having a human experience."

Think About It

Someone has remarked, "We are not responsible for the body we are born with, but we are responsible for the body we die with." Of course, individuals are born with DNA deficiencies, physical liabilities, or certain proclivities toward a certain disease. But as stewards of what we are given, we are to take care of our bodies. They are a gift from the Lord.

What This Means to You

The physical side of life has impact on the spiritual life and ministry you are called to fulfill. Do not exempt the physical side of your life from your daily and weekly schedules. But be careful you don't emphasize the less valuable physical pursuits to the downsizing or neglect of your pursuit of God. To do so is put your desire to glorify God in jeopardy.

Chapter 33
Work

What is the believer's attitude toward work? How can a man's work ethic escalate or diminish the light that shines from his or her life?

What the Bible Has to Say

Serve wholeheartedly as if you were serving the Lord, not men. (Ephesians 6:7)

Who do you work for? I asked that question in a Sunday morning worship service, and a couple of our people stated their place of employment. However, when I inquired of my neighbor Jeff Jones, he answered, "God." This is a landmark spiritual principle for the new believer to embrace. Work is no longer about earthly employers, but it is directed toward the Lord.

In Ephesians 6:5–9, Paul is addressing slaves who have become Christians and masters who have turned their lives over to Jesus Christ. It is estimated that in the Roman Empire there were approximately sixty million slaves. What were the expectations for a slave who now followed Jesus Christ? Many masters treated their slaves unfairly and often with brutality. Paul ups the ante for "saved slaves" and commands them to be obedient, respectful, and fearful of their masters. He challenges them to "obey your earthly masters . . . just as you would obey Christ."

Now that is a radical imperative. From the human standpoint you and I might say, "But Lord, my supervisor is a twerp" or "my supervisor underpays me" or "my foreman undervalues me." However, Paul, who was fully acquainted with the plight of the slaves, elevates the discussion to a new level: *work for your master as if you were serving Jesus Christ.*

Paul adds a convicting detail in Ephesians 6:6: "Obey them not only to win their favor when their eye is on you, but like slaves of Christ, doing the will of God from your heart." In other words, when the boss is not around, or when his or her eye is not watching, work as if he or she were standing beside you. Many employees follow the axiom, "When the cat's away, the mice will play." However, since the Lord never slumbers or sleeps, and since He is omnipresent, He is always watching.

The story is told about a father who took his son to the watermelon patch to steal watermelons. The father noticed his son was not snatching up any watermelons. He said, "Go ahead, no one is watching."

The son looked up at his dad, pointed to the sky, and said, "He is."

Since God is watching, we are to work and labor for Him. That could revolutionize the work force if followers of Jesus would remember who they are working for and who gives out the pay and rewards. You see, Paul placed a caveat in his instructional piece on work by adding, "The Lord will reward everyone for whatever good he does, whether he is slave or free." So there is a heavenly paymaster, and He is the Lord.

The apostle Paul goes on to address the masters—that is, the employers. Some of the masters of his time were accepting Jesus Christ as Lord and Savior. He reminded them that as masters they were not to threaten their employees. Instead, they should remember they have a Master in heaven, and He will show no favoritism. The master was also accountable to manage his workers in a fair and loving way, for he or she is also employed by the Lord (Ephesians 6:9).

Work is to be done in a spiritual way with the object not to just please earthly employers, who are sometimes a pleasure to work for and other times a pain. Workers are to see beyond their earthly overseers and see Jesus Christ as their ultimate employer.

Think About It

An old story tells of three workmen, building a cathedral. Each was asked, "What are you doing?"

The first answered, "I am chipping these stones."

The second replied, "I am earning wages."

The third had a much more inspirational attitude toward his work, for he responded, "I am building a great cathedral."

What This Means to You

The work of a believer is not only earthly and horizontal, but also eternal and vertical. A believer labors as working for Jesus. If you operate on this level, your work takes on a new dimension and becomes a tool of witness to those who work with you and those you work for in an employer-employee relationship.

Chapter 34
Parables

*So much of Jesus's teaching was given in parables, but what is a parable?
How are parables relevant to my life?*

What the Bible Has to Say

*The same day Jesus went out of the house and sat by the lake.
Such large crowds gathered around Him that He got into a boat and
sat in it, while all the people stood on the shore. Then He told them
many things in parables, saying: "A farmer went out to sow his seed."*
(Matthew 13:1–3)

The Greek word for parable (*parabole*) literally means "to cast
alongside." The traditional definition is "an earthly story with a
heavenly meaning." A helpful definition is harvested from Warren
Wiersbe, who wrote: "The parables are both windows and mirrors…
as mirrors they help you see yourself…as windows they help us see life
and God" (*Meet Yourself in the Parables*, p. 14).

There are approximately forty parables in the Gospels. Jesus used these
stories to give the listeners a better understanding of the Kingdom
of God.

Why should new believers study parables?

1. They are part of God's Word (2 Timothy 3:16–17)

2. Jesus employed them as a major part of His teaching

3. We think by converting abstract truths into concrete thoughts (word pictures)

4. They cover a broad spectrum of life (finances, forgiveness, judgment, love, prayer, relationships, rewards)

The parable of the soils provides an excellent example of how parables are written and the value they bring to our understanding. Jesus tells the story of a sower (Himself) who cast his seed (the Word of God) in four different soils (Matthew 13:1–9, 18–23). The point of the parable is to illustrate that the sower and seed are consistent, but it is the texture of a man's heart that rejects the seed or allows it to take hold and transform that man into a fruitful disciple.

The Master teacher described the four soils and also disclosed their meaning:

1. The firm soil represents a hard-hearted person who does not allow God's Word to penetrate his or her heart.

2. The rocky soil signifies a shallow-hearted person who reacts favorably to the truth of Jesus, but when opposition comes, then the truth of God's Word is quickly abandoned.

3. The thorny soil suggests a person with a strangled heart— choked by the anxieties of life and the allure of wealth that tempt him or her not to follow Jesus.

4. Finally, the fourth soil brings great promise to the story. The good soil is analogous to a person with an open and pliable heart who receives the Word of God, understands it, and applies it by producing fruit—that is, godly acts and deeds—for Jesus and the Kingdom of God. This leads to a closer walk with Jesus and a greater ability to share the gospel with others.

Although brief, this parable has tremendous teaching application. The story form creates an easy understanding of the teaching of Jesus.

Think About It

James Montgomery Boice wrote: "Other sections of the Bible give us grand theology. Some move us to grateful response to God. But the parables move through mere words and make us ask whether there has indeed been any real difference in our lives. Isn't that what we should expect since the parables come from the lips of Jesus? No one was ever better than Jesus at getting through pretense to reality" (*The Parables of Jesus*, p. 10).

What This Means to You

As you read the parables of Jesus, discover the overriding theme and instruction of each one. Then, deploy these parables in your church, home, and workplace to teach others.

Chapter 35
Fasting

What is fasting? What value does it have in my Christian life?

What the Bible Has to Say

After fasting forty days and forty nights, He [Jesus] was hungry. (Matthew 4:2)

The Scripture passage above is in reference to the temptation of Jesus Christ by the devil. Before the "championship bout" in the wilderness, Jesus exercised the spiritual discipline of fasting.

Fasting is abstaining from physical food in order to feed oneself with spiritual food, such as prayer and the Word of God. Notice this fasting did not prohibit the drinking of water, for the text does not mention that Jesus was thirsty. The practice of fasting by Jesus makes it an activity to consider since we are to walk as Jesus walked.

Our Master gives instructions regarding fasting in Matthew 6:16–18: "When you fast, do not look somber as the hypocrites do, for they disfigure their faces to show men they are fasting. I tell you the truth, they have received their reward in full. But when you fast, put oil on your head and wash your face, so that it will not be obvious to others that you are fasting, but only to your Father, who is unseen; and your Father, who sees what is done in secret, will reward you."

Two indisputable lessons emerge from this short passage: first, Jesus expects his followers to fast; second, no one around us should be able to detect we are fasting. The Pharisees, devout followers of the Law, made sure people knew they were fasting. History reveals that the Pharisees often fasted on Monday and Thursday because these were market days and a bigger audience would witness their piety and salute them (Arthur Wallis, *God's Chosen Fast*, p. 25).

There are several types of fasts mentioned in the Bible. A normal fast occurs when the individual refrains from all food. Typically, drinking water or juice is considered routine when fasting is observed. Humans can only survive for three to seven days without water. A partial fast is when the diet is limited, but the individual eats some food. An example of this is found in Daniel 1:12, when Daniel and three other Jews had "nothing but vegetables to eat and water to drink." An absolute fast is the avoidance of all food and water. This type of fast was done by Ezra for three days (Ezra 10:6); Esther and the Jews, who were threatened by annihilation (Esther 4:16); and Paul, when he was converted on the Damascus road and was blind for three days (Acts 9:9). Moses experienced a supernatural fast when he met God to receive the stone tablets which contained the Ten Commandments. Moses reported, "I stayed on the mountain forty days and forty nights; I ate no bread and drank no water."

Congregational fasts can be found in Joel 2:15–16, and national fasts appear several times in God's Word, such as in 2 Chronicles 20:3, Nehemiah 9:1, and Jonah 3:5–8 when, strangely enough, the pagan king of Nineveh proclaimed a fast in response to Jonah's proclamation that after forty days and nights God would overturn this great but wicked worldly city.

When we consider the varieties of fasting, and they are sprinkled throughout the Old and New Testaments, we can label fasting a valuable and viable exercise in our Christian walk.

Think About It

Cornelius Plantinga Jr. wrote: "Self-indulgence is the enemy of gratitude, and self-discipline usually its friend and generator. That is why gluttony is a deadly sin. The early desert fathers believed that a person's appetites are linked: full stomachs and jaded palates take the edge from our hunger and thirst for righteousness. They spoil the appetite for God" (*The Reformed Journal*, November 1988).

What This Means to You

Fasting may seem new or strange to you, but it is worth trying, especially since it was a habit of Jesus and many in the early church. It was written of senior citizen, Anna, in the Christmas Story, that "she never left the temple but worshiped night and day, fasting and praying" (Luke 2:37).

Chapter 36
Forgiveness

*Does the Lord expect us to forgive others who sin against us? What impact
does it have on my life if I forgive others or don't forgive others?*

What the Bible Has to Say

*For if you forgive men when they sin against you, your heavenly Father
will also forgive you. But if you do not forgive men their sins, your Father
will not forgive your sins.* (Matthew 6:14–15)

These two theme verses from Matthew immediately follow the Lord's
Prayer, which is the model prayer Jesus taught His disciples. Within
it are these words, "Forgive us our debts, as we also have forgiven our
debtors" (6:12). The word *debts* could be translated *sins*.

Believers must practice forgiveness, or they will disrupt God's grace
toward their own sins. So Matthew 6:14–15 more explicitly defines the
kingdom principle that the Heavenly Father's forgiveness is predicated
on the premise that we forgive others.

The Lord's forgiveness is magnanimously stated in Psalm 103:12,
"As far as the east is from the west, so far has He removed our
transgressions [sins] from us." In the New Testament, the word
forgive is made up of two Greek words which mean "to send away."

If the Heavenly Father is gracious toward those who wrong Him and break His commandments, we who call ourselves His children should act in like manner.

How many times should we forgive someone who has wronged us? Peter came to Jesus and asked that question: "Lord, how many times shall I forgive my brother when he sins against me? Up to seven times?" (Matthew 18:21). Considering that the Rabbis (Jewish teachers) taught forgiving a man three times is sufficient, it would seem to indicate Peter is generous in establishing his quota of seven times. However, our Lord raised the quota quite significantly when He answered Peter with these stunning numbers: "I tell you, not seven times but seventy times seven times" (Matthew 18:22).

Jesus followed His inflated reply with the parable of the unmerciful servant (Matthew 18:23–34). The story conveys that God forgives us of so many sins and He expects us to forgive others who offend us with their sins. The parable details the scenario of a king auditing his servant's accounts. A man owed the monarch 10,000 talents. Since a talent equaled nine years' work, that would establish the debt at 90,000 years' wages. This is an impossible debt to repay. The penalty leveled against the man would be that his wife, his children, and he would be sold. At this juncture, the indentured servant fell on his knees and begged for patience. The king, out of pity, pardoned him and forgave the debt, as monstrous as it was.

After the servant left, he found another servant who owed him 100 days' wages. He grabbed the servant, choked him, and demanded payment. The servant begged him with almost the same mannerisms and words that the forgiven servant had begged the king. However, the servant who had been forgiven of a debt too large to ever repay refused the plea and put him in prison. Some servants reported this demonstration of harshness to the king, and the unforgiving servant was called back and thrown into prison. Jesus summed up the parable with these words: "This is how the Heavenly Father will treat each of you unless you forgive your brother from your heart" (Matthew 18:35). The parable message is unmistakable: those who do not forgive will not be forgiven.

When people wrong us, is our response foreclosure on them or forgiveness? In his best-selling book, *The Freedom of Forgiveness*, David Ausburger writes, "Doing an injury puts you below your enemy; revenging an injury makes you but even; only forgiving sets you above."

Think About It

Amos and Andy, a comedy duo from generations ago, offer us a convicting story. There was a big man who would slap Andy across the chest whenever they met. Andy finally had his fill of this abuse and told Amos, "I am fixed for him. I put a stick of dynamite in my vest pocket and the next time he slaps me he is going to get his hand blown off." Unforgiveness not only hurts the offender, it also harms the offended.

What This Means to You

An unforgiving spirit is one of the most crippling liabilities to one who is seeking a healthy and holy relationship with God. Paul wrote to the church in Colossae, "Bear with each other and forgive whatever grievances you may have against one another. Forgive as the Lord forgave you" (Colossians 3:13).

Chapter 37
Missions

Is missions an optional or a nonnegotiable part of my Christian life?

What the Bible Has to Say

But you will receive power when the Holy Spirit comes on you; and you will be my witnesses in Jerusalem, and in all Judea and Samaria, and to the ends of the earth. (Acts 1:8)

The concept of missions is often given a lower priority in a believer's focus because he or she has seen many other individuals and churches attach a secondary value to it. However, the Bible is clear that "God so loved the world that He gave His one and only Son" (John 3:16). God has a worldwide vision for the saving of men and women. His view of salvation is global.

Consider the description of the great multitude in the final book of the Bible: "After this I looked and there before me was a great multitude that no one could count, from every nation, tribe, people and language, standing before the throne and in front of the Lamb. They were wearing white robes and were holding palm branches in their hands. And they cried out with a loud voice, 'Salvation belongs to our God, who sits on the throne, and to the Lamb'" (Revelation 7:9–10).

This assembly encompasses the planet, and the demographics are inclusive: every nation, tribe, people, and language. Since God's agenda is to spread His love and message around the world, then we should be supportive and involved in this enterprise.

Jesus, as He prepared to say good-bye to His disciples, left them with a command we call the Great Commission. He instructs His followers to disperse themselves to all nations. These words have motivated Christians throughout the ages: "Then Jesus came to them and said, 'All authority in heaven and on earth has been given to Me. Therefore go and make disciples of all nations, baptizing them in the name of the Father and of the Son and of the Holy Spirit, and teaching them to obey everything I have commanded you. And surely I am with you always, to the very end of the age'" (Matthew 28:18–20).

The impetus for missions is found in our Lord's deployment of His disciples with the word *go*. The extent of the going is clearly made explicit in the words *all nations*. Jesus's expectation is for a missionary force to spread His message to all people around the globe.

The word *missionary* is not in the Bible, but the concept is found in the meaning of the Greek word, *apostellos*, which refers to the senders and the ones who are sent with a message. This word, in noun and verb forms, appears over two hundred times in the New Testament. "Sending" and "being sent" are significant components of the early church.

Our English word, missionary, is derived from the Latin word, *mitto*. Actually, the Latin word focuses more on the people who are sent, while the Greek word encompasses the broader and deeper meaning of both those who support and send the messenger and those who are the carriers of the message. This is an important point: according to the original word, *apostellos*, the senders and the sent are *both* missionaries.

However, it is also critical to understand that some must go, and in our time the word missionary is most often used and defined this way. In the *Evangelical Dictionary of World Missions*, the sent missionary is defined in these terms: "These men and women are cross-cultural workers who serve within or without their national boundaries, and they will cross some kind of linguistic, cultural, or geographic barriers as authorized sent ones" (p. 645). This definition could describe a missionary in a neighborhood, community, region of the country, or another part of the world.

In order to achieve such a huge task, many believers must be willing to go, but all believers can be involved by praying and giving and sending men and women to the regions where the good news of Jesus needs to be heard and received.

This all-hands-on-deck mentality is illustrated at harvest time in Southeast Asia. In Cambodia, when the grain is ripe, the people live at the fields until the harvest is complete. Everyone participates—mothers and fathers, sisters and brothers, aunts and uncles, grandmothers and grandfathers—no one is exempt from helping with the harvest. The same should be true of those who claim to be disciples of Jesus Christ. Everyone is called to bring in the harvest of souls; no one is excluded.

Think About It

In *Missionary Messages*, A.B. Simpson tells of a missionary in Africa who witnessed for one day in a river village. The people were bitterly disappointed he could not stay longer. Two days later as he approached the village by boat, he observed people watching from the bank. They became wildly animated in their gestures and loud in their cries as they tried to convince him to come ashore. As he continued down the river, he could hear their bitter wailings, the lamentation of lost people who were seeking after God (p. 64).

What This Means to You

The missionary enterprise is at the very heart of God. It is a worldwide task that needs a worldwide workforce. Whether you become one who helps send or someone who is sent, it is imperative you are on the playing field and not a spectator in the stands.

Chapter 38
Healing

Is healing an authentic expectation in my walk of faith,
or is it something associated with cults and fanatics?

What the Bible Has to Say

Jesus went throughout Galilee, teaching in their synagogues, preaching
the good news of the kingdom, and healing every disease and sickness
among the people. (Matthew 4:23)

When healing is mentioned, eyes roll and minds turn to snake
charmers. Indeed, many have misused the doctrine and practice of
healing, and some have made fortunes by promoting their ability
to heal.

Nevertheless, make no mistake: Jesus engaged in a ministry of healing
and empowered his disciples to heal. Matthew 10:1 reports, "He called
his twelve disciples to him and gave them authority to drive out evil
spirits and to heal every disease and sickness." Jesus's healing power
was comprehensive: "every disease and sickness" (Matthew 4:23).

This ministry of healing was not happenstance. At the beginning of His
ministry, Jesus went into the synagogue in His hometown of Nazareth

and was handed a scroll. Luke provides this narrative: "Unrolling it, He found the place where it is written: 'The Spirit of the Lord is on me, because He has anointed me to preach good news to the poor. He has sent me to proclaim freedom for the prisoners and recovery of sight for the blind, to release the oppressed, to proclaim the year of the Lord's favor'" (Luke 4:18-19). In this inaugural reading for His ministry, He made an intentional reference to the healing ministry that would comprise a significant component of His ministry on earth.

Healing is probably one of the most misunderstood ministries of the Christian faith. Many have distanced themselves from the ministry of healing for a variety of reasons, including a reaction to abuses, a fear of being labeled fanatical, and a reluctance to explain a "failure" (when healing does not occur, even after earnest prayer). Regardless of these apprehensions, healing is found in both the Old and New Testaments. There are also verifiable healing stories in modern times.

After the great Exodus from Egypt, the Israelites heard the Lord's promise in reference to healing: "If you listen carefully to the voice of the Lord your God and do what is right in His eyes, if you pay attention to His commands and keep all His decrees, I will not bring on you any of the diseases I brought on the Egyptians, for I am the Lord, who heals you" (Exodus 15:26).

Isaiah 53 is a monumental chapter of prophesy that predicts the life and ministry of Jesus. In a graphic passage describing Jesus on the cross, the promise of healing is at the forefront as Isaiah details Jesus's horrible but healing death: "But He was pierced for our transgressions, He was crushed for our iniquities; the punishment that brought us peace was upon Him, and by his wounds we are healed" (53:5).

Matthew will report the fulfillment of this prophecy: "When evening came, many who were demon-possessed were brought to Him, and He drove out the spirits with a word and healed all the sick. This was to fulfill what was spoken through the prophet Isaiah: 'He took up our infirmities and carried our diseases'" (Matthew 8:16–17).

It is legitimate to take our requests for healing to the Great Physician in prayer. In the book of James, we find a practical prescription for those who are sick to pursue in their quest for healing: "Is anyone among you sick? Let them call the elders of the church to pray over them and anoint them with oil in the name of the Lord. And the prayer offered in faith will make the sick person well; the Lord will raise them up. If they have sinned, they will be forgiven. Therefore confess your sins to each other and pray for each other so that you may be healed. The prayer of a righteous person is powerful and effective" (5:13–16).

The basic elements in healing are as follows:

1. Recognize you are sick.

2. Call for the elders (spiritual leaders) of the church to pray over you and anoint you with oil in the name of the Lord.

3. Offer the prayer in faith that God can heal.

4. Healing will occur if it is God's will.

Jesus is a Healer. We must identify this reality and realize its potency in the healing of our body, mind, and soul.

Think About It

A.B. Simpson said, "Divine healing is not giving up on medicines or fighting against physicians or against remedies. It is not even believing in the prayer of faith or in the men and women who teach divine healing; nor is it believing the doctrine to be true. But it is really receiving the personal life of Christ to be in us as the supernatural strength of our body and the supply of our physical life. It is a living fact and not a mere theory or doctrine" (*The Word, the Work, and the World*, July/August 1887, p. 75).

What This Means to You

The Christian faith includes the doctrine of healing. This healing is not only for the soul but also for the mind and body. Don't neglect to pray and trust the Lord for healing. It is a viable tool in God's tool chest.

Chapter 39
Marriage: the Wife

*What does the Bible say about marriage and how can
this relationship remain healthy and holy?*

What the Bible Has to Say

*That is why a man leaves his father and mother and is united to his wife,
and they become one flesh.* (Genesis 2:24)

Wedding days are typically full of color, goodwill, a beautiful bride, a handsome bridegroom, and the highest of hopes built on the loftiest of dreams. But marriage is more than a thirty-minute ceremony or an expensive reception. Marriage is the primary illustration of the love between Jesus Christ and His church. It is a relationship with defined roles that create a complementary companionship. In my observation, marriages are failing at the same rate as they are succeeding. Can we change this tragic pattern? The answer is yes, if we follow the blueprint for marriage God planted in His Word. What follows is the pattern in Ephesians 5, which gives us the potential for maximum marriage.

As we survey the role of the wife, the starting point can be traced to Ephesians 5:18-20 and the "filling of the Spirit" which results in five actions: speaking, singing, making music, giving thanks, and submitting. In other words, the more the Holy Spirit controls our lives the greater the potential for healthy and holy relationships, especially in marriage.

The wife is to submit to her husband as the church is to submit to Jesus Christ (Ephesians 5:22–24). The origin and meaning of the word *submit* in the original language is "to arrange under." Its primary usage is military; we could define it as "to rank under." The armed forces operate under a hierarchy of leadership. Authority, not ability, is the key issue. The willingness to assume a task or to fulfill a role is at the heart of submission. I define submission as a voluntary yielding to authority which has been established by God as an act of obedience to His commands and as an expression of love to Him. In descriptive terms, the husband is the president of the home, and the wife is the vice-president.

In addition, the Ephesians passage, which functions like a marriage manual, gives two more instructions. The wife is to form with her husband a new physical organism in the flesh (5:31). The lack of this intimate physical relationship leads to temptation. Paul speaks explicitly of this temptation in 1 Corinthians 7:1–6. Also, the wife is to respect her husband. The word respect is *phobeo*, which can be translated "to fear, reverence, or to treat with deference."

In summary, there are four takeaways. The wife, who is analogous to the church, should pursue these four principles:

1. Be filled with the Holy Spirit, i.e., "under His control"

2. Be submissive to her husband

3. Be intimate physically with her husband

4. Be respectful of her husband

Only once in creation did God assess His work as "not good" and it was in reference to marriage. Genesis 2:18 reports, "The Lord God said, 'It is not good for the man to be alone. I will make a helper suitable for him.'" The wife is an essential partner in a complementary relationship that has been designed by the Creator.

Think About It

Family friend Adam Armstrong wrote this blog when his wife died in her early thirties: "At 3:25 p.m. today, September 2, Allie finished her race here with us. She came to the hospice care center late last night in need of platelets to help with her mouth bleeding. Soon she was complaining of trouble breathing and was largely sedated since then. The bleeding persisted and the breathing slowly gave out. She was surrounded by family and I got to walk my bride down the aisle to meet her Savior. To say I loved her seems a woeful understatement. She was incredible, beautiful, and godly."

This is the legacy of a godly wife and this is the expression of her husband who cherished her.

What This Means to You

Marriage may be diminished and joked about, but it is a bond the Lord used to convey the relationship between Jesus Christ and His church. Jesus is the bridegroom and the church is His bride. When your marriage is healthy and holy, it becomes a model of the love connection between our Savior and His people.

Chapter 40
Marriage: the Husband

What does the Bible say about marriage and how can
this relationship remain healthy and holy?

What the Bible Has to Say

That is why a man leaves his father and mother and is united to his wife,
and they become one flesh. (Genesis 2:24).

As we survey the role of the husband, the starting point can again be traced back to Ephesians 5:18–21. In verse 18, the origin of the husband's empowerment for serving his wife is anchored in the "filling of the Spirit" which results in five actions: speaking, singing, making music, giving thanks, and submitting. In other words, as with the wife, the more the Holy Spirit controls our lives the greater the potential for healthy and holy relationships, especially in marriage. The spiritual maturity of a man determines the capacity of his fulfillment of the husband's functions and ministries within home and the marriage.

The husband is to love (*agapao*) his wife as Jesus Christ loved the church (Ephesians 5:25). This is the highest bar for the man to aim for in his marital calling. The original word for love is defined by an unconditional commitment to his wife. This love corresponds to his wedding day vows, namely, "For better, for worse, for richer, for poorer, in sickness and in health, to love and to cherish, till death do us part."

Simply put, there are no conditions that should hinder his love for his wife. My wife was an Alzheimer's nurse. Faye would recount to me the different levels of commitment that husbands demonstrated to their wives as the woman proceeded through the stages of this debilitating disease. As the disease progresses the wife loses all memories of the relationship she had with her husband. She will arrive at a place where she has no recollection of the wedding, the honeymoon, the home, the children, or any meaningful component of what might have been a model marriage. Some men would continue to come and comfort their spouses, hold their hands, kiss them, read to them, and make an intentional effort to improve in any way possible their difficult lifestyle. Other men would stop coming and move on to their next relationship. The difference in responses is clear: for some men, there were no conditions that could shut off their love; for others, the condition of Alzheimer's had been a deal breaker.

A husband is to give himself for his wife, sacrificing for her daily. For the headship of a man is rooted in the example of Jesus, who was a suffering servant and put the needs of those He loved ahead of Himself (Matthew 20:28). The man stands between any threat that approaches his wife. He is the insulation, the protector; he makes her problems his problems.

As head of the home, the husband has the rare privilege of presenting his wife as a pure vessel who is holy and blameless before the Lord (Ephesians 5:22, 27). The husband is to be a purifying agent in his home, "to walk as Jesus did" (1 John 2:6). His lifestyle and the degree to which he imitates Jesus Christ will have a profound impact on the spiritual fitness of his wife.

He is to love his wife as he loves himself (Ephesians 5:28). Genesis 2:24 characterizes the husband and wife as one. It is a contradiction to love yourself and then not to love your spouse. Self-love is biblical. Jesus taught the importance of self-love by citing the commandment, "Love your neighbor as yourself," as second only to loving God with all your heart (Mark 12:31). If a man does not love himself, it will be extremely difficult, if not impossible to love his wife.

He is to be intimate with his wife (Ephesians 5:31). The act of physical love is associated with the survival and multiplication of the species: "God blessed them and said, 'Be fruitful and increase in number'" (Genesis 1:28). But intimacy is also connected to oneness in marriage and spiritual strength and health. Paul instructs married couples in 1 Corinthians 7:4–5, "The wife does not have authority over her own body but yields it to her husband. In the same way, the husband does not have authority over his own body but yields it to his wife. Do not deprive each other except perhaps by mutual consent and for a time, so that you may devote yourselves to prayer. Then come together again so that Satan will not tempt you because of your lack of self-control." The absence of intimacy can lead to spiritual vulnerability.

Four takeaways: The husband, who is analogous to the groom, Jesus Christ, should pursue these four steps:

1. He should demonstrate the sacrificial love of Jesus Christ for his bride.

2. He should pray and work to sanctify her life so he may present her pure to the Lord.

3. He is to love his wife as he loves himself.

4. He should be physically intimate with his wife.

Think About It

R. Kent Hughes tells a story of a Midwest farmer and his wife. While they were lying in bed, the funnel of the tornado suddenly lifted the roof off their house and sucked their bed away with them in it. When the wife began to cry the farmer tried to stop her tears but she exclaimed that she couldn't help it. She testified that she was so happy because "it was the first time they had been out together in twenty years" (*Ephesians: The Mystery of the Body of Christ*, p. 191).

What This Means to You

Through your marriage, you can illustrate the relationship that Jesus Christ has with His church. The world desperately needs to observe marriages where each spouse is for the other, and both spouses are for the Lord.

Chapter 41
Children

What does the Bible say regarding children and
the goals of parents in raising them?

What the Bible Has to Say

People were also bringing babies to Jesus to have Him touch them. When
the disciples saw this, they rebuked them. But Jesus called the children
to Him and said, "Let the little children come to me, and do not hinder
them, for the kingdom of God belongs to such as these. I tell you the truth,
anyone who will not receive the kingdom of God like a little child will
never enter it." (Luke 18:15-17)

The theme verses convey Jesus's high regard for children. Parents were
making a sincere effort to bring their children to Jesus, and they were
met with resistance from our Lord's own disciples. Apparently the
disciples did not place a premium on these little individuals. However,
Jesus extended a sincere welcome to the children and highlighted the
truth that those who seek the kingdom of God must come like little
children, humble and full of trust.

Children are a gift from God. Psalm 127:3 asserts that "Sons are a
heritage from the Lord, children a reward from Him." David wrote in

Psalm 139 that God was already working while he was developing in his mother's womb, "For You created my inmost being; You knit me together in my mother's womb. I praise You because I am fearfully and wonderfully made; Your works are wonderful, I know that full well. My frame was not hidden from You when I was made in the secret place, when I was woven together in the depths of the earth, Your eyes saw my unformed body; all the days ordained for me were written in Your book before one of them came to be" (13–16).

Even before birth, God is working in the womb of the mother to create the child. Jeremiah was appointed as a prophet while he was in his mother's womb (Jeremiah 1:5) and John the Baptist leaped in his mother's womb when he heard Mary, the mother of Jesus, greeting his mother, Elizabeth (Luke 1:41, 44).

A child does not automatically turn out to be a stellar follower of Jesus. In fact, a child is bent toward evil and not good as stated in Proverbs 29:15: "The rod of correction imparts wisdom, but a child left to himself disgraces his mother." If a child is left to go his own way, he will not choose the right path. That is the reason Proverbs 22:6 challenges and commands parents to "Train a child in the way he should go, and when he is old he will not turn from it." There must be cultivation of faith and morality. There must be discipline and consequences applied to the child when he or she disobeys God's commands and breaks God's laws.

Likewise, there needs to be affirmation and encouragement when the child chooses wisely and displays a godly choice. "Children are wet cement," Anne Ortlund writes in a book by the same title. She asserts that when a child is complimented, good behavior is reinforced. For example, if a little boy brings his mother a dandelion, she has a choice to either condemn him for bringing a weed or bless him with gratitude for bringing such a beautiful yellow creation.

William Barclay, in his insightful book, *Educational Ideals of the Ancient World*, outlined the three goals of Jewish parents in respect to their children. They are to know God, to marry properly, and to have a vocation. These goals encompass the priorities of a righteous and rewarding life and focus on our faith, our family, and our work. If these goals are accomplished, a child has been trained correctly and the value of his life will be greatly enhanced.

Think About It

Children Are a Treasure from the Lord

Halls ring with echoes of laughter
Long after they've come and gone
For the memory of a tiny face and playful grin
Still brings a smile, reminding us again
That children are a treasure from the Lord

Songs sweetly sung by the cradle
Prayers whispered just before bed
And we taught them "Jesus loves you" in a simple song
And we pray they won't forget their whole life long
Children are a treasure from the Lord
Those bright and trusting eyes
Seem to take us by surprise
And they see what others older seem to miss
May the gift of faith they hold

Grow as they grow old
May they always know God will never let them go

At six they're beginning their school days
Sixteen and they're driving the car
And at twenty-one we'll let them go on their first date
But of course they'll be at home in bed by eight
Yes, children are a treasure from the Lord

Homes ring with echoes of laughter
Long after they've come and gone
And just knowing that our children really love the Lord
Is a faithful parent's passion and reward
Yes, children are a treasure from the Lord
Children are a treasure from the Lord
Yes, children are a treasure from the Lord

Words and music by Jon Mohr, Phil Naish, and Greg Nelson Copyright 1989. Used by permission.

What This Means to You

In The *Expositor's Bible Commentary* (Vol. XI, p. 80), A. Skevington Wood declares, "Disobedience to parents is a symptom of a disintegrating social structure, and Christian families have a particular responsibility not to contribute to the collapse of an ordered community."

If you are a parent, raising champions for Christ is one of your highest privileges and greatest responsibilities.

Chapter 42
Christmas

What is the meaning of Christmas and how can I
observe it appropriately as a believer?

What the Bible Has to Say

She (Mary) will give birth to a son, and you are to give Him the name
Jesus, because He will save His people from their sins. (Matthew 1:21)

Every year it is the world's biggest birthday party. We call it Christmas, the "mass" of Christ. The birth of the Savior prompted incredible joy during that first Christmas celebration. Mary gave us the "Magnificat," a mother's praise song for the Holy One of God, whose seed had been planted in her womb. The shepherds discovered night shift could be exciting as a special constellation dotted the sky that canopied the cradle of the King that inaugural Christmas Eve. Yes, it was the birthday of a majestic monarch. The Messiah, a deliverer, had entered the realm of the earth, born of a woman. God's Son had put on skin. This baby was the prophets' special project, the one they had foretold, the one predicted to change the world. Nothing would ever be the same—history would be more than ever "His-story."

Over two millennia have passed and what has become of the birthday of the King? A.W. Tozer made this dark appraisal of our contemporary Christmas as he protested the holiday's drift from its original intent: "In our mad materialism we have turned beauty into ashes, prostituted every normal emotion and made merchandise of the holiest gift the world ever knew. Christ came to bring peace and we celebrate His coming by making peace impossible for six weeks of each year. Not peace but tension, fatigue and irritation rule the Christmas season" (*The Warfare of the Spirit*, p. 60).

Dr. Thomas Holmes, with his colleagues at the University of Washington, developed the now famous stress scale which measures the stress certain life events bring into our lives. Christmas received a rating of twelve, almost half the value of remodeling a home, rated at twenty-five, and almost one-third the stress of pregnancy, which was rated at forty. Christmas could now be properly termed "Christ-mess."

The first Christmas, however, opened up the blossoms of joy in the lives of men and women like a warm sun shining on our dogwood tree in the spring. There is a natural manifestation of beauty and fulfillment when humanity worships divinity and when the sons of Adam and the daughters of Eve are engaged with the Son of God. The first Christmas wrote new chapters of gladness into the diaries of those Jewish men and women, and even those Gentile Magi rejoiced when they finally found Jesus and His family by following a unique star. You and I can embrace the Christmas season with our hearts full of God's love and our lips reciting the goodness of the Eternal God.

Give one gift to Christ this Christmas:

- Forgive someone.

- Let go of a bad habit.

- Begin a holy habit.

- Love someone who doesn't love you.

- Accept the circumstances you are in by faith.

- Worship Him.

Think About It

Holiday comes from the words *Holy Day*. Long ago these days were granted so workers could go to church and worship. May your next Christmas truly be a Holy Day as you rearrange your priorities for the glory of the Father, Son, and Holy Spirit.

What This Means to You

As a believer, you can embrace Christmas, for it commemorates the coming of the King. Don't fill up all the white space in your calendar with so much chaos and stuff that you emerge a weaker disciple rather than a more dynamic one. Joy should be a by-product of your next Christmas celebration.

Chapter 43
Easter

How is Easter more relevant to me now that I am a follower of Jesus Christ?

What the Bible Has to Say

The angel said to the women, "Do not be afraid, for I know that you are looking for Jesus, who was crucified. He is not here; He has risen, just as He said. Come and see the place where He lay." (Matthew 28:5–6)

Easter Week commemorates Jesus's pathway to His death on the cross for our sins, His burial in a borrowed tomb, and His resurrection from the dead on Sunday. These events, culminating in the resurrection, are relevant to you for the following reasons:

1. Because Christ rose on Sunday (Matthew 28:1-6), the Christian church worships on that day. The early church began this model (1 Corinthians 16:2; Acts 20:7; Revelation 1:10), while the Jewish people had their Sabbath, their day of rest and worship, from sundown on Friday to sundown on Saturday. We celebrate the resurrection fifty-two times a year.

2. Because Jesus predicted his death and resurrection, we know he is a truth teller. Especially important is His prediction that

He would rise from the dead (Matthew 16:21; Mark 9:31). C.S. Lewis put Jesus's predictions in these terms: "A man who was merely a man and said the sort of things Jesus said would not be a great moral teacher. He would either be a lunatic—on the level with a man who says he is a poached egg—or he would be the devil of hell. You must take your choice. Either this was, and is, the Son of God, or else a madman or something worse."

3. Because Jesus has defeated death, we can face this final enemy with confidence and not fear. Death is no longer an undefeated bully waiting to confront you. Prior to raising his friend Lazarus from the dead, Jesus announced, "I am the resurrection and the life. He who believes in Me will live, even though he dies, and whoever lives and believes in Me will never die." (John 11:25–26). Death has been defeated. The sting of death has been removed and replaced by the victory through our Lord Jesus Christ (1 Corinthians 15:56–57).

4. Because we have hope, we do not grieve as those who have no hope (1 Thessalonians 4:13). Sylvia Bellinger, one of my parishioners, wrote these words which were read at her funeral: "But to mourn for those who died is misplaced sorrow. There should be rejoicing on their behalf because the pain is ended, the sorrow is gone. A bright new world of perfection awaits them." Certainly we lament and weep over the loss of a loved one, but their death is a promotion to a place prepared for them by Jesus.

5. Because Jesus is alive, we move forward in mission and ministry with a spring in our step and great courage in our hearts. This is

why preaching and living out our faith have great purpose and value (1 Corinthians 15:14–24). Christianity is rooted in history. Our authority and power are anchored in facts, not fantasy.

If Jesus is alive, death becomes the doorway to life. The grave in the garden tomb becomes the cornerstone of our hope and our graves take on the nature of a waiting room and not a home.

If He has been raised, then we shall be raised because "He is the firstfruits of those who have fallen asleep" (1 Corinthians 15:20).

Think About It

A farmer understands that he must surrender a seed to the ground in order to see the birth of a crop. Our Lord taught about death and resurrection by sharing this illustration: "Unless a kernel of wheat falls to the ground and dies, it remains only a single seed. But if it dies it produces many seeds" (John 12:24). He highlighted that the kernel must perish in order to yield a crop. So, our death leads to our eternal life with Him. And the kernel of His life surrendered at the cross led to a harvest of souls.

What This Means to You

Death is for a moment. Eternal life is forever.

Chapter 44
Death

*How does the fact that I am a Christian change
my view of death and how I face it?*

What the Bible Has to Say

*Where, O death, is your victory? Where, O death, is your sting? . . . But
thanks be to God. He gives us the victory through our Lord Jesus Christ.*
(1 Corinthians 15:55, 57)

Death is usually associated with defeat. It is the cessation of physical
life as we know it: the heart stops beating; brain wave activity ceases.
But the Christian faith looks at death differently. In fact, at some
funerals the preacher will say, "Our brother has been promoted."

I have attended many funerals and my observation is that the
nonbelievers cry and wail desperately, while the believers, though
grieving, often manifest an assurance and peace about the passing of
their loved one—if he or she had a personal relationship with Jesus
Christ. Death for the disciple of Jesus is not a hopeless end, but an
endless hope.

Death is an appointment we will have on our daily planners, because
dying is a part of living. In his old age David made this observation:

"I am about to go the way of all the earth" (1 Kings 2:2). We may miss a doctor or dentist appointment, but we will not miss that appointment. Hebrews 9:27 frames our death in these terms: "Man is destined to die once."

How then do we face death with courage and faith? Paul, in 1 Corinthians 15:26, labels death as the final enemy, but he also predicts its defeat when he writes, "The last enemy to be destroyed is death." In other words, when the dust of death surrounds us, we can be confident that it will not win the battle. It is a defeated foe because of the resurrection of Jesus Christ from the dead and because God has the authority and power to do the same miracle for us.

Peter said we are "aliens and strangers in this world" (1 Peter 2:11), and Paul asserted, "Our citizenship is in heaven. And we eagerly await a Savior from there, the Lord Jesus Christ, who, by the power that enables Him to bring everything under His control, will transform our lowly bodies so that they will be like His glorious body" (Philippians 3:20–21).

Yes, our bodies do decay on our earthly journey, but we are awaiting a new body. Paul said our earthly bodies (he called them earthly tents) were being destroyed, but he added that we possess a heavenly dwelling, an eternal house (body) in heaven that will not be destroyed (2 Corinthians 5:1–5).

One of the most poignant moments in the New Testament is found in the shortest verse of the Bible, John 11:35, which is comprised of only two words: "Jesus wept." The occasion was the death of his friend, Lazarus.

Jesus had been summoned with this message, "Lord, the one you love is sick" (John 11:3). But rather than going immediately to Lazarus's sick bed, he waited four days. Many scholars believe he waited for that period of time because the Jews thought the soul remained near the body for three days. Jesus was going to resurrect Lazarus from the dead, and He did not want anyone claiming death had not been final. In fact, He told His disciples, "Lazarus is dead, and for your sake I am glad I was not there, so that you may believe." (John 11:14-15).

When Martha ran out to meet Jesus, she bemoaned the reality of Lazarus dying and stated, "If you had been here, my brother would not have died" (John 11:21).

Jesus then told her, "Your brother will rise again" (John 11:23).

She did not understand it would be imminent and by faith stated, "He will rise again at the last day" (John 11:24).

Jesus—fully aware He would raise Lazarus from the dead—replied, "I am the resurrection and the life. He who believes in Me will live, even though he dies; and whoever lives and believes in Me will never die" (John 11:25-26). Death wins for a microsecond; the believer wins forever.

Think About It

Natalie A. Sleeth wrote the following hymn in 1985 while reflecting on the death of a friend. Her husband asked that it be sung at his funeral. I have requested that it be read at my funeral.

Hymn of Promise

In the bulb there is a flower; in the seed, an apple tree;
In cocoons a hidden promise: butterflies will soon be free!
In the cold and snow of winter there's a spring that waits to be,
Unrevealed until its season, something God alone can see.

There's a song in every silence, seeking word and melody;
There's a dawn in every darkness, bringing hope to you and me.
From the past will come the future; what it holds, a mystery,
Unrevealed until its season, something God alone can see.

In our end is our beginning; in time, infinity;
In our doubt there is believing; in our life, eternity,
In our death, a resurrection; at the last a victory,
Unrevealed until its season, something God alone can see.

Copyright 1986 Hope Publishing Company.
Used by permission.

What This Means to You

The life you live begins with birth and ends with death. Jesus promises you that death boasts too loudly of what it can do to you. Because He lives, you will live also.

Chapter 45
Resurrection

Now that I am a believer, how should I face death?

What the Bible Has to Say

Jesus said to her [Martha], "I am the resurrection and the life. He who believes in Me will live, even though he dies; and whoever lives and believes in Me will never die. Do you believe this?" (John 11:25–26)

Every time our family drove from Shippensburg to Chambersburg, Pennsylvania, we read a large billboard that reminded every traveler there is an appointment that absolutely no one will miss. The sign contained the text of Hebrews 9:27 KJV, "It is appointed unto men once to die, but after this the judgment." This was a rather blunt announcement (especially in light of the fact that we often stopped at that point in the trip for ice cream), but it is a reality we need to face. Death, like birth, is a necessary landmark on the human journey.

How does the Bible describe death? Paul labels it the final enemy in 1 Corinthians 15:26: "The last enemy to be destroyed is death." Death is a gladiator that will stand in our way between time and eternity. As a pastor I have observed that death sometimes comes quickly, in an event such as a massive heart attack or a catastrophic car accident. At other times, death comes slowly, through cancer or some other fatal disease. But whether fast or slow, death is final as far as our earthly existence. Our hearts stop beating; our brain waves cease; we take our final breath.

Yet, before Paul finishes this chapter, he removes the gloom and exchanges it for the glorious outcome that awaits every follower of Jesus Christ. He speaks of the resurrection of the dead. He contrasts a body that perishes with the imperishable body we will be given following death. Furthermore, he proclaims, "Death has been swallowed up in victory" (1 Corinthians 15:54).

Paul follows this triumphant statement by comparing death to the sting of a bee, which hurts us, but is not fatal. He asks, "Where, O death, is your victory? Where, O death, is your sting? . . . But thanks be to God! He gives us the victory through our Lord Jesus Christ" (15:55, 57).

Death for the believer is not just pain but a promotion into the presence of God. Again we consult Paul for a tremendous declaration of our eternal bond to the love of God: "For I am convinced that neither death nor life, neither angels nor principalities, neither the present or the future, nor any powers, neither height nor depth, nor anything in all creation, will be able to separate us from the love of God that is in Christ Jesus our Lord" (Romans 8:38–39).

Think About It

I have been asked why a sheaf of wheat is often placed in or on the casket at a funeral. The answer comes in John 12:24 from the lips of

Jesus: "Unless a kernel of wheat falls to the ground and dies, it remains only a single seed. But if it dies, it produces many seeds." Farmers understand this analogy well, for they must surrender their seeds to the ground if a crop is to grow and be harvested. So it is with our death: we are like a kernel that is surrendered in death, only to bloom into eternal and everlasting life.

What This Means to You

Death for the believer is only for a moment; it is a comma, not a period.

Chapter 46
The Bema Seat

*What is the Bema Seat and how does it pertain
to me as a believer in Jesus Christ?*

What the Bible Has to Say

*For we must all appear before the judgment seat [Greek: bema] of Christ
that each one may receive what is due him, for the things done while in
the body, whether good or bad.* (2 Corinthians 5:10)

As you learn about the Christian life through your study in the Bible
you may hear discussions on rewards. Though some teachers may
have an aversion to the subject, it is clear in the New Testament that
rewards are an important part of the biblical record. In fact, in the last
chapter of the Bible these words are recorded from the lips of Jesus:
"Behold, I am coming soon! My reward is with me, and I will give to
everyone according to what he has done" (Revelation 22:12). When
Jesus teaches the principles of the kingdom in what has been termed
the Beatitudes (Matthew 5:3–12), He concludes with this summary
statement: "Rejoice and be glad, for great is your reward in heaven, for
in the same way they persecuted the prophets who were before you."

In Romans 14:10 and 2 Corinthians 5:10, the words *judgment seat*
appear. These two words are the translation of one word, *bema*. The

Gospels employ this word in Matthew 27:19 and John 19:13 to refer to an elevated platform where a Roman judge or ruler would issue decisions and verdicts.

Paul would raise this term to a new level, a spiritual plane. The great apostle was familiar with the athletics of the Greek culture. At many of these games, athletes would compete for a prize under the eyes of judges who would make sure the rules were followed. The judges would escort the winners to the platform called the bema, where the rewards were presented. Paul converted this athletic analogy to the spiritual battle or contest where the believers would appear before Jesus Christ to receive their rewards. The judge at the worldly Bema Seat awarded winners; he did not punish losers. The Bema Seat is for believers to be judged by their Lord and subsequently receive rewards for their service and work.

A significant passage is found in 1 Corinthians 3:10–15, where Paul details the assessment of the Christian's works. Some are deemed valuable; others are graded as of little value or worthless. Paul's passage reveals the different outcomes: "By the grace God has given me, I laid a foundation as a wise builder, and someone else is building on it. But each one should build with care. For no one can lay any foundation other than the one already laid, which is Jesus Christ. If anyone builds on this foundation using gold, silver, costly stones, wood, hay or straw, their work will be shown for what it is, because the Day will bring it to light. It will be revealed with fire, and the fire will test the quality of each person's work. If what has been built survives, the builder will receive a reward. If it is burned up, the builder will suffer loss but yet will be saved—even though only as one escaping through the flames."

Please notice what these verses are saying: a believer will not lose his salvation ("will suffer loss but yet will be saved"); instead, the rewards of believers will be different based upon the quality of their deeds. A different premium is placed on "gold, silver, and costly stones" as compared to "wood, hay, or straw." Our works do not save us—we are saved by the gracious gift of God's Son—but we will be judged and rewarded for those precious acts that we did in the name and power of Jesus Christ.

Think About It

"Bema Seat," penned by Bob Hartman and recorded by Christian rock group Petra conveys the message of the judgment seat:

> *When our labors all retire*
> *There will be a trial by fire*
> *Build your treasure, pass the test*
> *Or will it burn up with the rest?*
>
> *You can build upon a firm foundation*
> *With your building in dilapidation*
> *When it all comes down to rubble*
> *Will it be wood, hay, or stubble?*
>
> *Precious stones, gold and silver*
> *Are you really sure?*
>
> *And we all will stand at the Bema Seat*
> *All will be revealed, it will be complete*
> *Will there be reward in the fiery heat*
> *When we see our lives at the Bema Seat? Yeah*

Every talent will be surely counted
Every word will have to be accounted
Not a story will be left untold
We will stand and watch the truth unfold

Every score will be evened
Nothing to defend

And we all will stand at the Bema Seat
All will be revealed, it will be complete
Will there be reward in the fiery heat?
When we see our lives at the Bema Seat?

Every building will be shaken
Every motive will be tried
He'll give reward to the faithful
Will you receive or be denied?

And we all will stand at the Bema Seat
All will be revealed, it will be complete
Will there be reward in the fiery heat
When we see our lives at the Bema Seat?

What This Means to You

Your service to God will not be forgotten or overlooked; it will be evaluated and rewarded by the fairest and most impartial judge of all time.

Chapter 47
Heaven

Is heaven a real place? How does the Bible describe it?

What the Bible Has to Say

But our citizenship is in heaven. And we eagerly await a Savior from there, the Lord Jesus Christ. (Philippians 3:20)

Heaven is simply defined as the dwelling place of God. The prophet Isaiah recorded these words: "Heaven is my throne" (Isaiah 66:1). You may recall that the Lord's Prayer begins with these words, "Our Father in heaven" (Matthew 6:9). When Jesus ascended, Peter tells us that He "has gone into heaven and is at God's right hand" (1 Peter 3:22).

The good news is that we will also go to heaven to be with our Lord. In John 14:2–3, Jesus makes this promise: "My Father's house has many rooms; if that were not so, would I have told you that I am going there to prepare a place for you? And if I go and prepare a place for you, I will come back and take you to be with Me that you also may be where I am."

Heaven is a real place, not a fantasy world or a myth; it is the future residence of all who accept Jesus Christ as Lord and Savior, whose names are written in the *Lamb's Book of Life* (Revelation 21:27).

What are some of the descriptions of heaven? There is no nighttime in heaven (Revelation 21:25). In fact, there is no need of the sun, because the heavenly city will receive its light from God's glory (Revelation 21:23). Heaven is a holy city (Revelation 21:2), and it measures about 1,400 miles in length, breadth and height, which are all equal (Revelation 21:6, 16). All kinds of colorful, precious stones are a part of the makeup of this incredible place, and its streets are pure gold (Revelation 21:18–21). God's people will worship the Lord (Revelation 22:3), and His people will see the face of Jesus (Revelation 22:4). Can you imagine the moment you will look into the eyes of the Son of God?

Because we exist in a fallen world, and brokenness embraces all of our lives through such conduits as disease, divorce, deception, and destruction, we look forward to a place of immeasurable beauty and peace. Many of us have watched the slow or sometimes speedy demise of a loved one with cancer, looked into the eyes of parents who buried their baby, heard stories of job loss, or witnessed disasters, whether man-made or natural.

In contrast, heaven is a place to look forward to with heightened anticipation. John's vision in the book of Revelation paints a picture of the new paradise with these comforting words: "Then I saw a new heaven and a new earth, for the first heaven and the first earth had passed away, and there was no longer any sea. I saw the Holy City, the new Jerusalem, coming down out of heaven from God, prepared as a bride beautifully dressed for her husband. And I heard a loud voice from the throne saying, 'Look! God's dwelling place is now among the people, and He will dwell with them. They will be His people, and God Himself will be with them and be their God. He will wipe every tear from their eyes. There will be no more death or mourning or crying or pain, for the old order of things has passed away'" (Revelation 21:1–4).

This picture that John, inspired by the Holy Spirit, has placed before us is a sight for sore eyes and sore hearts. In *The Last Battle*, C.S. Lewis wrote, "I have come home at last! This is my real country! I belong here. This is the land I have been looking for all my life, though I never knew it till now . . . Come further up, come further in."

Amen!

Think About It

> *Think of . . .*
>
> *Stepping on shore, and finding it heaven!*
>
> *Of taking hold of a hand, and finding it God's hand.*
>
> *Of breathing new air, and finding it celestial air.*
>
> *Of feeling invigorated, and finding it immortality.*
>
> *Of passing from storm to tempest to an unknown calm.*
>
> *Of waking up, and finding it Home.*
>
> — Author Unknown, published in The *Best Loved Poems of the American People*, 1936. Hazel Felleman, editor.

What This Means to You

Death for the believer is not an *Omega*, an end; rather it is an *Alpha*, a new beginning. You have so much to look forward to and so little to leave behind. Heaven is before you, and it is one spectacular place to reside—forever.

Chapter 48
Hell

What is hell and how does the Bible describe it? Who will inhabit it?

What the Bible Has to Say

Do not be afraid of those who kill the body but cannot kill the soul. Rather, be afraid of the One who can destroy both soul and body in hell. (Matthew 10:28)

The Scriptures relate that hell is an actual place where the wicked are punished forever. The descriptions of hell in the Bible are frightening. Some of the characterizations include unquenchable fire, the lake of fire and brimstone, and where the worm does not die.

In the parable of the talents, Jesus tells of a servant who didn't invest his master's money, but buried it in the ground. When the master learned of this, he said, "Throw that worthless servant outside into the darkness, where there will be weeping and gnashing of teeth" (Matthew 25:30).

When Jesus is speaking of the King's decisions regarding the righteous and the unrighteous He makes a clear distinction that the wicked "will go away into eternal punishment, but the righteous to eternal life" (Matthew 25:46). It is important to note the word for *eternal* is the exact same word for both the best of rewards and the worst of punishments in that passage.

The actual word for hell in the New Testament is *gehenna*. It appears twelve times, eleven of which occur in the first three Gospels—Matthew, Mark, and Luke. Every time the word is used it comes from the lips of Jesus. Gehenna is a valley south of Jerusalem where the Jews sacrificed their children to the false god, Molech (1 Kings 11:7). King Josiah designated it to be a place where dead bodies were deposited and burned (2 Kings 23:13,14). It literally was a garbage dump where contents burned and smelled up an area of that region. So, Gehenna with its historic ties to apostasy, its continually burning debris, and its reputation as a garbage dump, became the most frequently used term for hell, the eternal place of the lost.

Jesus made it clear that hell was not prepared for humans, but "prepared for the devil and his angels" (Matthew 25:41). However, Jesus also spelled out that those who did not accept Him, who rejected His offer of forgiveness and salvation, would be cursed and sent into the eternal fire (Matthew 25:41). This destiny was—and is—to be avoided at all costs.

In Mark 9, Jesus prescribes cutting off your hand or foot if it causes you to stumble and end up in hell (Mark 9:43, 45). He further recommended that if your eye was causing you to sin, you should pluck it out "because it is better to enter the kingdom of God with one eye than to have two eyes and be thrown into hell" (Mark 9:47). Jesus is not literally telling people to cut off their hand and foot, or to pluck out their eyes. Rather, He is exaggerating the point to illustrate the need for individuals to avoid sin and pursue righteousness, which leads to His blessings and His rewards.

One particularly gruesome rendering of Scripture nails down the critical point that men and women should avoid hell at all costs. This passage is found in Revelation 14:9–11: "A third angel followed them and said in a loud voice: 'If anyone worships the beast and his image and receives his mark on their forehead or on the hand, he, too, will drink of the wine of God's fury, which has been poured full strength into the cup of His wrath. He will be tormented with burning sulfur in the presence of the holy angels and of the Lamb. And the smoke of their torment rises for ever and ever. There is no rest day or night for those who worship the beast and its image, or for anyone who receives the mark of his name.'"

Think About It

In *The Great Divorce*, C.S. Lewis wrote, "There are only two kinds of people in the end: those who say to God, 'Thy will be done,' and those to whom God says, in the end, 'Thy will be done.' All that are in hell, choose it. Without that self-choice there could be no hell. No soul that seriously and constantly desires joy will ever miss it. Those who seek find. To those who knock it is opened."

What This Means to You

Heaven will be a more beautiful and better place than anyone could imagine. Hell will be a more awful place than anyone could imagine. If you have chosen Jesus and His offer of salvation, you have chosen wisely. You have chosen heaven. If you have neglected and rejected Jesus, your nightmares will be the best of your future, for the reality of hell will far exceed your darkest imaginations.

Chapter 49
The Devil

Is the devil or Satan a real person?
If so, how does that affect my Christian walk?

What the Bible Has to Say

Then Jesus was led by the Spirit into the desert to be tempted by the devil.
(Matthew 4:1)

The Holy Bible is emphatic that there is a real devil. Many individuals, when they think of the devil, conjure up a picture in their mind of a bizarre-looking creature with horns and a long tail who holds a pitchfork in his hand. This caricature was developed in the Middle Ages to diminish people's fear of someone who really frightened them. We should not underestimate this fallen angel who has brought destruction, misery, and sin to millions of human lives.

Many names are used to describe the head of the demon world. The term *devil* appears only in the New Testament. The name *Satan* is a Hebrew word meaning adversary (see Job 1:6). Other names are used to describe the leader of the dark side. He is called the serpent, the ruler of this world, the prince of the power of the air, the evil one, and Beelzebub, which means "Lord of the flies."

The description of the devil or Satan in the Bible paints a dark and ominous picture. He is the one who lured Eve into disobeying God's orders in the Garden of Eden (Genesis 3:1–6). He is characterized as having "sinned from the beginning" (1 John 3:8). Scripture likens him to a roaring lion in 1 Peter 5:8: "Be self-controlled and alert. Your enemy the devil prowls around like a roaring lion looking for someone to devour."

Satan knows and can quote the Bible as evidenced by His tactics in tempting Jesus. He uses the unbeliever to his advantage: "You followed the ways of this world and of the ruler of the kingdom of the air, the spirit who is now at work in those who are disobedient" (Ephesians 2:2). He is so deceitful and deceptive that he can appear as an angel: "For Satan himself masquerades as an angel of light" (2 Corinthians 11:14). The devil is intelligent, powerful, and has tremendous resources at his disposal.

The believer should not take the devil lightly, but neither should he or she panic before him. He is a defeated foe. Jesus, the champion of the righteous, overcame the devil's temptations to lure Jesus into sin. It is noteworthy that Jesus's ammunition was to quote three Scriptures from the book of Deuteronomy. Satan's power is limited as is evidenced in Job when God puts restrictions on his activity and purview. The mission of Jesus was "to destroy the works of the devil" (1 John 3:8 NLT), and the devil will be thrown into the lake of fire: "And the devil, who deceived them, was thrown into the lake of burning sulfur, where the beast and the false prophet had been thrown. They will be tormented day and night for ever and ever" (Revelation 20:10).

All believers should take heart in this fact: "You, dear children, are from God and have overcome them, because the one who is in you is greater than the one who is in the world" (1 John 4:4). Paul warned: "Our struggle is not against flesh and blood, but against the rulers, against the authorities, against the powers of this dark world and against the spiritual forces of evil in the heavenly realms" (Ephesians 6:12). This is not a natural war but a supernatural war, and fortunately we have the spiritual assets to win it.

Think About It

Reflect on this poem by Alfred J. Hough, written in 1885:

> *Men don't believe in the devil now,*
> *as their fathers used to do;*
> *They've forced the door of the broadest creed*
> *to let his majesty through.*
> *There isn't a print of his cloven foot*
> *or fiery dart from his brow*
> *To be found on earth or air today,*
> *for the world has voted it so.*

> *Who dogs the steps of the toiling saint*
> *and digs the pits for his feet?*
> *Who sows the tares in the fields of time*
> *whenever God sows the wheat?*
> *The devil is voted not to be,*
> *and of course, the thing is true;*
> *But who is doing the kind of work*
> *that the devil alone can do?*

We are told that he doesn't go about
as a roaring lion now;
But whom shall we hold responsible
for the everlasting row
To be heard in home, in church and state,
to the earth's remotest bound,
If the devil by unanimous vote
is nowhere to be found?

Won't someone step to the front forthwith
and make their bow and show
How the frauds and crimes of a single day
spring up? We want to know!
The devil was fairly voted out,
and of course, The devil's gone;
But simple people would like to know
who carries the business on.

What This Means to You

You are standing with two choices. Choose Jesus Christ and you will receive righteous and eternal, everlasting life. Choose the devil and you will harvest sin and eternal death. Follow Jesus—it is a narrow road but its destination is worth the sacrifice.

Chapter 50
The Second Coming of Christ

What are some of the details of the Second Coming of Jesus?
What impact does it have for living the Christian life?

What the Bible Has to Say

They were looking intently up into the sky as He was going, when suddenly two men dressed in white stood beside them. "Men of Galilee," they said," why do you stand there looking into the sky? This same Jesus, who has been taken from you into heaven, will come back in the same way you have seen Him go into heaven." (Acts 1:10–11)

The Lord Jesus Christ was predicted to come the first time by many prophets in the Old Testament. Isaiah, the writer of the longest book in the Old Testament, featured many such prophecies regarding the coming of Jesus. Micah even prophesied the place of Jesus's birth as tiny Bethlehem over seven hundred years before He was born in that city, which is also the birthplace of David, the mighty king of Israel. Although many centuries passed before Jesus fulfilled these prophesies, in the fullness of time He did come.

Jesus predicted His second coming when He spoke these words, "So you must also be ready, because the Son of Man will come at an hour when you do not expect Him" (Matthew 24:44). The Master unfolded a parable to emphasize the uncertainty of the time, but also the definite reality that He will come again. This parable of the ten virgins tells the story of ten women who went out to meet the bridegroom. Five virgins were wise because they took oil in jars to light their lamps so they could see the way to the wedding banquet. Five virgins were foolish because they carried no oil with them.

The bridegroom delayed in coming and announcing his great banquet, but at midnight it was heralded that "Here's the bridegroom! Come out to meet him!" (Matthew 25:6). When the bridegroom arrived, the five virgins who had oil were able to light their lamps and go into the banquet. The foolish virgins who had no oil went to buy some, but by the time they returned, the door was shut.

Jesus made the point of readiness clear: "Therefore, keep watch, because you do not know the day nor the hour" (Matthew 25:13). *Be ready* is the warning of Jesus.

The time of Jesus's coming has often been forecast throughout the centuries and even in modern times. This type of predicting is discouraged by Jesus Himself. In Acts 1:7, He instructed His disciples, "It is not for you to know the times or dates the Father has set by His own authority." This reinforced an earlier teaching that He gave to them in Matthew 24:36 regarding His second coming: "No one knows about that day or hour, not even the angels in heaven, nor the Son, but only the Father." The type of crystal ball predicting of the day of Jesus's return is foolish, and will only hurt the legacy and the witness of the one engaging in it.

Again, the message reads loud and clear: *be ready.* Paul's writings in 1 Thessalonians frame Jesus's coming in the terms of a "thief in the night" (5:2). Typically, a thief does not announce to the homeowner when he is going to break into the owner's house and take his possessions. His entry is a surprise. Jesus's coming is comparable to this unpredictable thief. Again, the clarion call is to be ready.

The certainty of Jesus's words should produce some positive outcomes in our lives of faith. Paul wrote in 1 Thessalonians 4:18, "Therefore encourage each other with these words." In Titus 2:13, Paul stipulated that this waiting on Jesus's coming allows us to embrace a "blessed hope" while we wait for "the glorious appearing of our great God and Savior, Jesus Christ."

Think About It

Jesus's return visit to the Planet Earth is mentioned over three hundred times in the New Testament. The Christian is commanded to prepare for this event, for it could happen at any moment, at the next tick of the clock.

What This Means to You

You should live within the shadow of the second coming of Jesus. He is coming, make no mistake; the mistake is not being ready for this climactic event.

Chapter 51
Slaves to Jesus Christ

If slavery is such an oppressive concept,
why am I as a believer designated a slave?

What the Bible Has to Say

You have been set free from sin and have become slaves to righteousness.
(Romans 6:18)

The new believer in Jesus Christ is destined to run into some of the paradoxes that are ingrained in the Christian message. The last are first, the poor are rich, the weak are strong, and in the theme verse, the free are slaves. Slavery in our culture and in the world's history has been viewed as an abusive and inhumane system, but this metaphor is employed often to define and describe the life of a Christian.

The word for slave in the original Greek is *doulos*. It appears over 120 times in the New Testament, and in forty-four of those occurrences it is used in a spiritual sense. Romans 6 includes several verses that refer to believers as slaves. The first reference points out that our slave relationship with sin has been altered: "For we know that our old self was crucified with Him [Jesus] so that the body of sin might be done away with, that we should no longer be slaves to sin" (Romans 6:6).

In other words, before our life in Jesus, we were controlled by sin and we obeyed its wayward commands and suggestions. We served our sinful nature.

Romans 6:16 presents the two slave options: "Don't you know that when you offer yourselves to someone to obey him as slaves, you are slaves to the one whom you obey—whether you are slaves to sin [and Satan], which leads to death, or to obedience, which leads to righteousness?"

You cannot escape being a slave, but you have two options: you will either obey sin and Satan, with an undesirable and final outcome of death; or you will obey the Lord and His Word, with a preferable outcome of righteousness and a final outcome of heaven.

Someone or something will be your master. The theme verse and Romans 6:22 speak of our emancipation and liberation from sin. These verses then describe our new "slave relationship" with righteousness and Jesus Christ. Slavery is transformed when we receive Jesus Christ as personal Lord and Savior.

Some new Christians understand that Christ becomes their Savior when they accept salvation, but they don't think he becomes their Lord until later in the relationship. Scripture does not give us this option. At the moment of our salvation He is both Savior and Lord, He is Master, He holds all the papers and deeds.

Acts 2:21 explains that "everyone who calls on the name of the Lord will be saved." Jesus is Lord at the initial call. When the Philippian jailer rushed in to see if Paul and Silas had escaped following a great earthquake, he asked them a pointed question: "Sirs, what must I do to be saved?" (Acts 16:30). Their answer highlighted the Lordship of Jesus: "Believe in the Lord Jesus, and you will be saved" (Acts 16:31). At the jailer's conversion, Jesus was Lord.

In Paul's great masterpiece to the church at Rome, he passed on these requirements for salvation: "That if you confess with your mouth, 'Jesus is Lord,' and believe in your heart that God raised Him from the dead, you will be saved" (Romans 10:9).

Confessing that "Jesus is Lord" is a nonnegotiable action to be saved. You see, as a believer you do not make Jesus a mere addition to your life; instead, you are to live in total submission to Him. Because He is our Lord and Master, we are to exercise a singular devotion to Him. We are to carry out His will, not our own. This is a radical commitment, but it is the commitment we are commanded to make. He is the Master; we are the slaves.

Jesus "gave Himself for us to redeem us from all wickedness and to purify for Himself a people that are His very own, eager to do what is good" (Titus 2:14). Did you catch the reality that Jesus possesses us? We are His property, His possession. Our identity resides in Him. Our allegiance belongs to Him.

First Corinthians 6:19–20 frames our faith relationship with Jesus in these terms: "You are not your own; you were bought at a price." In the first century, masters bought slaves; in the Christian faith, Jesus has bought us from our sins by His atoning sacrifice, so we could be His precious possession and live a life of righteousness.

Think About It

William Barclay, in his book *The Letters of James and Peter*, made this assertion: "As Christ is Lord, so the Christian is a slave, even bond slave, owing unquestioning obedience. Paul explicitly compares spiritual with literal slavery (e.g. Colossians 3:22–24), speaks of slave-marks and seals of Christ's possession, and works out in detail the conception of the Christian as purchased, belonging to the Lord" (p. 39).

What This Means to You

Jesus Christ has transformed the concept of slavery from one of bondage to one of blessing. Praise Him that you are His slave and a precious possession of His heart.

Chapter 52
Continuing the Walk

In his book, *The Way*, E. Stanley Jones cited the illustration of a teacher who was talking to slum children and asked what they thought of Jesus. A little Italian boy answered, "Jesus is the best photograph that God ever had took" (p. 46).

The apostle Paul would agree with this child's assessment. In Colossians 1:15 he wrote, "Christ is the visible image of the invisible God" (NLT). In the book of Hebrews, Paul also would chime in with his concurrence, "The Son is the radiance of God's glory and the exact representation of His being" (Hebrews 1:3). So, when Jesus invites us to follow Him, we have the great privilege of following the Son of God who perfectly represents his Heavenly Father. *Therefore, we become imitators of God when we are J-Walking.*

It is crucial to understand that following Jesus is a long-term proposition. The nickname for the early Christians was "people of the Way." Saul, before he was converted and his name changed to Paul, asked the high priest for letters to the synagogues in Damascus, "so that if he found any there who belonged to the Way, whether men or women, he might take them as prisoners to Jerusalem" (Acts 9:2). In Ephesus there was a huge riot and the Scriptures report, "About that time there arose a great disturbance about the Way." (Acts 19:23). Jesus gave Himself the designation in John 14:6, "I am the way and the truth and the life. No one comes to the Father except through Me." He also talked about a narrow way in the Sermon on the Mount, that indicated the path that His followers would take and find life, "Enter through the narrow gate. For wide is the gate and broad is the road that leads to destruction, and many enter through it. But small is the gate and narrow is the road that leads to life, and only a few find it" (Matthew 7:13-14).

Following Jesus is not a one-time, one-moment, one-day decision. This adventure lasts from the time of accepting Jesus Christ throughout a lifetime. You have studied and hopefully are now embracing some of the theology and then living out the biology of the Christian life. We are all pilgrims pursuing a productive path on earth that will one day allow us to reach heaven, the ultimate destination. Keep leading others to Jesus and teaching them to live and love like Him. Keep J-Walking and you will experience the Abundant Life. "The one who says he abides in Him ought himself to walk in the same manner as He walked (1 John 2:6 NASB).

References

Ammer, Christine. 2003. *The American Heritage® Dictionary of Idioms*. Houghton Mifflin Harcourt Publishing Company.

Augsburger, Dad. 1970. *The Freedom of Forgiveness*. Chicago: Moody Press.

Barclay, William. 1974. *Educational Ideals in the Ancient World*. Grand Rapids: Baker Book House.

Ibid. 2003. *The Letters of James and Peter*. Louisville: Westminster John Knox Press.

Boice, James Montgomery. 1983. *The Parables of Jesus*. Chicago: Moody Press.

Bonhoeffer, Dietrich. 1959. *The Cost of Discipleship*. New York: Macmillan.

Brown, Colin, ed. 1979. *The New International Dictionary of New Testament Theology*. 3vols. Grand Rapids: Zondervan.

Bunyan, John. 2007. *Pilgrim's Progress*. Chicago: Moody Publishers.

Coleman. Robert E., ed. 1970. *One Divine Moment*. Old Tappan, New Jersey: Spire Books.

Cook, Robert A. 1949. *Now That I Believe*. Chicago: Moody Press.

Felleman, Hazel. 1965. *Poems That Live Forever*. New York: Doubleday.

Friesen, Garry. 1980. *Decision Making and the Will of God*. Portland: Multnomah Press.

Hartman, Bob. 1983. *"Bema Seat."* Dawn Treader Music. Used by permission: License No. 589472.

Holmes Thomas, and Richard Rahe. *1967.* "The Social Readjustment Rating Scale." *J Psychosom Res. 11 (2): 213–218.*

Hough, Alfred. 1885. *"Don't Believe in a Devil."* Quoted in a New Zealand Newspaper.

Hughes, R. Kent. 1990. *Ephesians: The Mystery of the Body of Christ*. Wheaton: Crossway Books.

Lehman, Frederick M. 1917. *"The Love of God"* published in *Songs That Are Different*. Pasadena: n.p.

Lewis, C.S. 2001. *Mere Christianity*. New York: HarperCollins.

Ibid. 1966. *Surprised by Joy*. San Diego: Harcourt, Brace, Jovanovich.

Ibid. 2001. *The Last Battle: The Chronicles of Narnia*. New York: HarperCollins.

Ibid. 2015. *The Great Divorce*. New York: HarperOne.

Logan, Robert E., and Neil Cole. 1995. *Raising Leaders of the Harvest*. St. Charles, Illinois: Church Smart Resources.

Miller, Donald. 2003. *Blue Like Jazz*. Nashville. Thomas Nelson.

Nelson, Greg, Jon Mohr and Phil Nash. 1989. "*Children Are a Treasure from the Lord.*" Greg Nelson Music. Used by permission: License No. 589455.

Moreau A. Scott. 2000. *Evangelical Dictionary of World Missions*. Grand Rapids: Baker.

Mote, Edward. 1834. "*My Hope is Built.*" London: The Gospel Magazine.

Pinocchio. Walt Disney Productions, Released by RKO Pictures, 1940.

Plantinga Jr., Cornelius. November 2008. *The Reformed Journal*.

Sleeth, Natalie A. 1986. *Hymn of Promise*. Carol Stream, Illinois: Hope Publishing. Used by permission.

Simpson, A. B. 1987. *Missionary Messages*. Camp Hill, Pa.: Christian Publications.

Swindoll, Charles. 1983. *Standing Out*. Portland: Multnomah Press.

Ibid. 1887. "*The Word, The Work, and the World.*" July/August.

Tozer, A. W. 2009. *The Knowledge of the Holy*. New York: HarperOne.

Ibid. 1993. *The Warfare of the Spirit*. Camp Hill, Pa.: Christian Publications.

Tripp, Paul. 2008. *How to Be Good and Angry* [video]. Philadelphia: Paul Tripp Ministries.

Wagner, C. Peter. 1979. *Your Spiritual Gifts Can Help Your Church Grow*. Ventura, California: Regal.

Wiersbe, Warren W. 1983. *Meet Yourself in the Parables*. Wheaton: Victor Press.

Wood, A. Skevington. Quoted in Gaebelein, Frank E., general editor. 1976. *The Expositor's Bible Commentary*. Vol. XI. Grand Rapids: Zondervan.

Topical Index by Chapters